To Bob

Enjoy

Herd About Town

Animal's Influence on Man

Robert C. Layton

Black Rose writing™

First printing

ISBN: 978-1-61296-569-7

PUBLISHED BY BLACK ROSE WRITING

www.blackrosewriting.com

Printed in the United States of America

Suggested retail price $16.95

Herd About Town is printed in Adobe Garamond Pro

I dedicate this book to the unsung heroes in the development of mankind. Be amazed by the incredible contribution of animals.

CONTENT

Herd About Town

Prelude

While, through the centuries, animals have consistently been our greatest friends and our most patient mentors, we humans are sometimes their best friends and sometimes their worst enemies. This dichotomy in our behavior arises from the fact that humans were dealt the winning ticket in life's lottery. By virtue of our intelligence, we are the dominant species on this earth. We may choose to be merciful or choose to be brutal and animals for the most part are helpless to change the outcome that we decide for them.

Even though there are some people who are cruel and uncaring toward animals, and some few who actually seem to delight in their suffering, the vast majority of people feel a deep and natural sense of empathy with animals. That empathy is reflected in our laws, albeit lightly enforced, that criminalize cruelty to animals. I believe that the empathy most of us feel for animals arises from a recognition that other species share with us; the senses of joy and pain and the same love of life and family. Somewhere inside us, we recognize that we are actually animals ourselves and that, as sentient beings, all animals share a fundamentally similar life experience.

In this book, Bob Layton shows us the many fascinating ways in which that fundamental affinity between humans and other species of the animal world has played out over centuries. This book provides both an entertaining and an educational overview of the myriad ways in which we humans have learned from animals, benefited from them and relied on them, both for help and for comfort. Mr. Layton shows us how much animals have contributed to our languages, our mythology and our wellbeing. They provide us with companionship in good times and solace in bad ones. They have been our partners and our guides and we have counted on them for so much. Examples abound like Balto the sled dog who saved the town of Nome, Alaska by carrying the desperately needed serum to treat a diphtheria epidemic through white-out conditions in 1925. Most of us have our own examples when, in times of sadness or loss, we have thrown our arms around our loving and non-judgmental pet. We owe our animal companions a great deal.

I was very grateful to be invited by Bob Lavton to write this Prelude because his book serves to enhance our understanding and appreciation for the ways in which we and other animals are, and have always been, mutually supportive partners in our life experience on this earth. That appreciation can only serve to help people value the lives of animals more and treat them with greater mercy and compassion. And, that advances the cause of animal welfare and my organization.

I lead an organization whose role is to protect, save and advocate for animals. Our mission is simply stated as being "to promote and practice the principle that every life is precious." We are a no-kill private humane organization because we believe that is not ethical to end the lives of companion animals who are healthy or have an ailment that is treatable.

Because the Richmond SPCA only shelters dogs and cats, many people believe that our mission ends there but that is far from the truth. We advocate for the interests of all animals and stand up for their protection from cruelty and harm. In fact, our organization was founded in the late nineteenth century with a focus on advocating for the protection of horses rather than dogs and cats.

1 am-asked frequently by foundations and other institutional donors how the Richmond SPCA provides human services (the suggestion being that this will be the only route to receiving support). There is an easy answer to this question: because pets vastly improve the quality of human lives and the work of the Richmond SPCA brings enormous happiness, companionship and comfort to people. However, the better response is more subtle and may be gleaned from the fascinating information provided in this book. People and animals are, and have been for many centuries, mutually supportive. Animals have proven themselves time and again to be the best friends we could ever hope for. They do not have rights but, rather, it is we who have great responsibilities arising from the dominion over other animals that we have been given. It is our responsibility to behave in the ways that affirm our role as compassionate stewards and that

reflect our gratitude and respect for the wonders of their long and essential friendship to us. In this book, Bob Layton carries us to that inescapable conclusion.

And, so in truth, everything about what the Richmond SPCA does provides a human service, just as does this book, because the greatest possible service to humanity is to strengthen our society's moral core, increase its sense of compassion for the powerless and voiceless, awaken its humility and reduce its culture of self-centeredness. Thanks to our animal companions, we are never alone. Our debt to them is great.

~Robin Robertson Starr, SPCA CEO

Introduction

Man emerged as the ultimate animal but he had a lot of help getting there. In much earlier times birds and animals of all kinds played an important part in mankind's survival. Man hunted and trapped them for his food, and made use of their skins and feathers for his clothing. But as time passed he began to appreciate the different species and to take notice of their various habits and skills.

Just as music speaks an international language, animals have a way of communicating with people of all tongues. Their methods are intelligent, reliable, and often humorous. Animals are so agreeable they ask no questions, make no criticisms and are so loyal we sometimes forget the marvelous, yet unheralded, influence they have had on man throughout the ages.

From the time we get up in the morning until we lay our head on the pillow for a night of rest we encounter the effect of animal persuasion. At breakfast we may enjoy eggs accented with toast spread with honey and washed down by a glass of milk. If the weather dictates a coat you could enjoy the warmth of a wool coat or a down filled jacket. If leisure is your plan a carriage ride pulled by a fine horse or a ride in the saddle could be in order. Should your day include work or play in one of the world's many deserts you may wish to enlist the services of a camel.

We are aware of members of the animal kingdom assisting the sightless and their support as companions and pets, but there is more. The following pages seek to give animals recognition for setting the standard for so many of the things we do in our daily lives.

Farmers are indebted to burrowing animals that loosen the soil for planting and thankful for dogs herding the cows and sheep. These canines are also useful for guarding the hen house. Horses and oxen assist with the plowing and cats are useful in keeping destructive varmints population down. Birds and squirrels are valuable for their role in planting seeds and aiding the dispersal of nut trees and conifers. The eggs from chickens, ducks, and goose and the milk from cows are valuable contributors to the success of the farm.

Those in police work make good use of dogs in crowd control and their ability to sniff out drugs and criminals. Rescue personnel use dogs to look for survivors or corpses. Animals are effective in finding kidnap victims, lost hikers, children that have wandered off and others in need. Their loyalty keeps them on track is spite of suffering from paw cuts, burns, dehydration, burning eyes and psychological stress. In the aftermath of 911, more than 350 dogs scoured the rubble at the World Trade Center.

The K9 corps of our military is in a class of its own. Their long term service in so many functions with our armed services is legendary. A great number of other members of the animal kingdom play important roles is assisting these protectors of our freedom.

Contribution to our language is perhaps where animals have had their most profound effect. An abundance of words, expressions, clichés, proverbs, and phrases employ animal names adding color, depth, and richness to our communication. Some are based on an animal's appearance; others on their habits. Some are based on a positive feeling about the animal; others on a negative reaction. Some are based on true characteristics of an animal; others, on false beliefs. Various expressions have a clear, definite origin; others, an uncertain origin buried in the dim past. From all this we find myths and superstitions with animal persuasion on weather prediction, medical remedies, safety measures, luck factors, and matters of life and death.

Our personality traits are very often explained by animal comparisons. The early bird gets the worm, a bull in a china shop, eat like a pig, gentle as a lamb, and monkeying around are among the more familiar animal sayings. Loose as a goose, go hog wild, strong as an ox, wise as an owl, and red as a lobster, are also common ways to describe mankind through animal vernacular..

Animal symbolism is significant in paintings, statues and heraldry all over the world. Animals are found on coins across the globe. It may be enough to know that Shakespeare used over 4,000 references to animals in his character portrayals

Birds and animals of all kinds came to be represented in cave drawings, and to decorate the walls of ancient tombs and buildings. History records their influence on man many years before the birth of Christ. Today, we depend on animals for meat, milk, wool, and leather; we worship our household pets as important companions; we appreciate our beasts of burden that are helpful in farming and in many places for transportation.

Perhaps in America it started with the Indians. The American Plains Indians believed that the character of whatever they ate became a part of their character. For example, if they ate grizzly bear, they would become as mean and as brave as the bear. If they ate venison, they would become as swift as the deer. If fox or wolf were consumed, they could attain the wily and clever traits of these beasts.

Every now and then this led to a little cannibalism on a very minor scale. If a very ambitious warrior killed an exceptionally skilled enemy, then the courageous heart of the loser might be eaten so that it might live on in the victor. This belief made the Indian very diet-conscience; for he knew that the foods he consumed would be reflected in his character and abilities.

There seems to be a reason for everything in nature. Large or small, beautiful or strange, each plant and animal has a purpose. Each has an effect on something else which sooner or later has an effect on us. It appears animal's influence on our lives is a major part of that plan. Man has taken his cue from animals for many of our habits shaped, languages developed, and traditions formed.

Herd About Time Animal's Influence on Man attempts to report on these impacts in a thought provoking format that gives credence to the outstanding contribution creatures and critters have made to mankind. The arrangement revolves around many of our favorite creatures providing pleasurable reading while affording a learning experience. Readers of all ages will gain a clearer understanding and appreciation of the animal kingdom as trailblazers for humanity. The process is succinctly summed up in Job 35:11 as follows, "Who teacheth us more than the beasts of the earth, and instructeth us more than the fowl of the air."

Meet Our Mentors

Taxonomists currently recognize about 1.25 million animals with a variety of characteristics. They range in size from viruses and microscopic worms to blue whales; they live in virtually every region of the planet, from boiling-hot vents in the ocean floor to clouds high in the stratosphere. Some live but a single day while, others like the clam, survive 400 years. Very few make it past 20 years.

These potential instructors are very different in appearance, habitat, and instincts and can be found in equatorial rainforests, deserts, rivers, seas, cave, even miles underground in minute cracks in the rocks. Their numbers are ever being altered as new species are found and others become extinct.

Included in the breakdown are 400,000 beetle species leading the invertebrates and 30,000 species of fish that head the number of vertebrates.

Although there is found a varying degree of intellect in these creatures, out of the enormous numbers only man has developed reading, writing religion, science, technology and language. Separating them into classifications, before entering their classroom, may be helpful to gain some sort of order.

Mammals, a group that includes humans is our first exploration. Mammals are endothermic (warm blooded) vertebrates. Most are covered with insulating fur. Female mammals produce milk to feed their young. They are found everywhere on Earth and most give birth to well-developed young.

Bats are the only flying mammals. They are generally nocturnal. The majority of bats are small insect-eaters like the bumblebee-sized hog-nosed Kitti, the world's smallest mammal. Bigger fruit bats eat fruit and nectar, and find food using their large eyes.

The Primates group includes apes, monkeys, lemurs, bush babies, and humans. Most primates live in social groups in tropical and subtropical forests. The majority are agile climbers with long limbs and flexible grasping fingers and toes. Primates also have forward-facing eyes and large brains compared to their body size.

Odd-toed ungulates have either one or three working toes such as the rhinos, horses, zebras, and tapirs. All are herbivores and many species are fast movers that live on open plains. Odd-toed Ungulates walk on the tips of their toes, each of which is capped with a hard hoof.

Even-toed Ungulates is a separate group of hoofed mammals, including deer, cattle, camels, hippos, and pigs, usually have two hoof-tipped toes. These herbivores have large cheek teeth to grind tough vegetation and may also have large, four-chambered stomachs inside where bacteria and tough plants are digested.

Carnivores are hunters and scavengers that feed largely on meat. Carnivores include tigers and other members of the cat family, along with wolves, foxes, otters, and bears. Most are fast-moving, locate prey by using their good senses of sight, smell, and hearing, and have sharp teeth to grip and cut flesh.

Marsupials are animals with a pouch that include kangaroos, koalas, and opossums. Female marsupials give birth to tiny immature young that complete their development inside their mother's pouch.

Lagomorphs include rabbits and hares. They are fast-moving ground dwellers that eat grasses, soft shoots, and tree bark. Their large ears are highly sensitive, and their bulging eyes provide all-around vision. At the first sound or sight of danger, they use their long hind legs to escape predators.

Echidnas and duck-billed platypus are monotrermes found in Australasia. They are the only mammals to lay eggs. After hatching, their young feed on milk. The platypus is a good swimmer and probes for prey in the beds of streams and lakes. Spiky echidnas mostly feed on ants and termites.

Insectivores are insects and other small animals. Unfortunately, they are the preferred prey of mammals. Insectivores are typically small, solitary nocturnal animals that have sharp teeth and depend on their senses of smell and touch to find food. Shrews and hedgehogs are included in this class. Males are insectivores adapted for life underground.

Rodents are a large class with more than 2,000 species. They comprise the largest mammal group and are found everywhere except Antarctica. The class includes mice, rats, squirrels, beavers, and porcupines. To gnaw tough foods they have two pairs of sharp incisor (front) teeth, which do not wear down because they never stop growing.

Cetaceans include whales, porpoises, and dolphins. They are mammals that spend their entire lives in water. They have a hairless body propelled by a powerful tail fin and steer by flippers.

The next category, birds, is able to cover an amazing range of habitat as a result of their ability to fly. They can be found on cliff faces, rain-forests, canopies, and on mountains. These high-flyers have streamlined, lightweight bodies with wings that are covered and insulated by feathers. Their boneless beaks vary in shape and size according to their diet and feeding method. Nearly 10,000 species of birds are divided into 29 orders.

Perhaps one of the least popular classifications is reptiles. Alligators, cobras, tortoises, and geckos are among this group of vertebrates. Most reptiles live on land, and all have tough, scaly skin that stops them from drying out, even in hostile desert habitats. Many have powerful jaws and sharp teeth to grab unwary prey. Some lay eggs with leather shells, although some produce live young. Reptiles are ectothermic (cold-blooded). They bask in the sun's heat to warm up and seek shade to cool down.

Lizards make up more than half of the 8,000 reptile species. Most are agile, fast-moving hunters. They include skinks, chameleons, slow worms, Gila monster, and the Komodo dragon.

Worm lizards live in hotter parts of the world. Most have no limits and all burrow underground, pushing trough soil or sand using their blunt-shaped heads. Worm lizards have fair simple eyes and feed on insects and worms that they find by touch.

Snakes are close relatives. Although all are carnivorous only about one-tenth are venomous. Adders, cobras, and rattlesnakes are in the minority that immobilizes their prey by injecting venom, or poison through special teeth called fangs. Some nonvenomous snakes are still to be avoided. Constrictors, such as corn snakes and python, grab their quarry using sharp teeth then wrap themselves around their the prey until it suffocates. Then like all snakes they swallow their victim whole.

We can't overlook turtles and tortoises in this category. The bodies of these reptiles are protected by a hard shell. Turtles live in the sea and fresh water, while tortoises live on land. All lay their eggs on land with marine species migrating across oceans to do so. Both lack teeth but their jaws have sharp edges to cut food. Tuataras are also a burrowing reptile. Found on islands off New Zealand they are the sole survivors of an ancient group related to snakes and lizards. They are nocturnal and can live more than 100 years.

Amphibians spend part of their life on land and part in water, where they eat and breed. Females lay shell-less eggs, which hatch into swimming larvae called tadpoles that breathe using gills. As they grow into adults, amphibians develop lungs and they can also breathe through their skin. There are three groups of amphibians; frogs and toads, salamanders and newts, and the less familiar caecilians.

Turning to other water instructors we find fish in lakes, rivers, and oceans. Fish are vertebrates that have adapted to a wet life. Their streamlined bodies are protected with scales, and fins that propel and steer. Three types of fish roam the waterways; the jawless fish such as lampreys, cartilaginous fish such as sharks and rays, and bony fish; the highest and most diverse fish group.

Swimming nearby are the echinoderms. This group includes starfish, sea urchins and their relatives like the feather star, sea cucumber, brittle star and sand dollar. These sea farers have no distinct head. Instead the body is divided into five equal parts arranged around a central disc, with the mouth usually on the underside. The body is supported by an internal skeleton made of chalky plates covered by spiny thin skin. An internal hydraulic system pumps water into and out of sausage-like tube feet each tipped with a sucker that project from the body and are used for movement.

In the same pool we find crustaceans that range from tiny brine shrimps to large spider crabs that are part of the 50,000 species. Crustaceans have a hard external skeleton known as the exoskeleton or cuticle, jointed limbs, two pairs of sensory antennae and compound eyes on stalks. Their heads and thoraxes are often covered by a shield or carapace. The better known crustaceans are crabs, krill, shrimps, and barnacles.

The daddy of all water-dwellers may be Mollusks. With over 100,000 species, ranging from garden slugs to pearl-bearing oysters and terrifying giant squid. Despite their differences mollusks share common features. They all have a soft body often protected by a hard chalky shell and feed using a roughened strip called a radula. They have a muscular foot and breathe through gills. Most belong to the gastropods; that includes snails and slugs.

Sponges, jellyfish and coral are some of the simplest members of the animal kingdom. They belong to three phyla-animals that feed by filtering food from the water. Cnidarians include hydrozoans, jelly fish, corals and sea anemones. All have stinging tentacles that immobilize and trap prey. Ctenophores, also known as comb jellies, are related to the cnidarians.

We can't forget arachnids; spiders, mites, ticks, scorpions and tarantulas. These mostly land-dwelling predators use venom to disable their prey, then douse it with digestive enzymes and suck up the resulting liquid. The arachnid body has two parts-cephalothoraxes at the front and an abdomen at the rear.

Attached to the cephalothoraxes are a pair of fanglike mouthparts called pedipalps that are either leg-like or claw-like, and four pairs of walking legs. In spiders, the abdomen contains silk-producing glands.

We worm out of this chapter by reporting on the squirmy crawlers. The term worm is a general one used to describe invertebrates that have long, soft bodies and usually no legs. Worms are found in a range of habitats including soil, tropical forests, lakes, rivers, and the sea. Flatworms are the simplest worms and have flattened ribbon like bodies. Annelids have bodies divided into segments. Other worm groups include peanut worms and velvet worms.

This is the faculty and man has been the student. Not all have held class or given instruction but the magnitude of their collective influence is wide-spread. The following chapters will identify how this kingdom has had a lasting effect on so much that we do.

Animals appearing in Mentors.

alligator
barnacles
beaver
bird
caecilian
chameleon
cnidarians
coral;
crabs
ctenophores
dolphin
fish, jelly, rays, sharks, star,
frog
gecko
gila monster
hedgehog
komodo dragon
lizard
mice
mollusks
newt

oyster
platypus
porcupine
porpoise
rat
salamander
sand dollar
sea cucumber
shrew
shrimps
skunk
slug
snail
snakes, adder, cobra, constrictor, corn, python, rattle
sponge
squid
squirrel
tadpole
ticks
toads
tortoise
tuataras
turtle
urchin
whale
worm

Animal Ant-idotes

Animals may never replace doctors but they could be setting up medical practices any day. Already a significant number of human patients are benefiting from animal therapy. Many legitimate methods are being utilized. Treatment using animal support can be found in residential centers, acute care facilities, hospice settings, special needs classrooms, homes, in mental health programs, and juvenile detention centers.

Animals often become the silent therapist allowing patients to unload their problems and concerns without fear of being judged. Animals are always good listeners, never give bad advice, and offer unconditional love and affection. You can count on them to be supportive.

The results are well documented. The presence of pets is beneficial in improving the quality of life in many areas. Comfort during periods of grief, motivation for therapy following injury or surgery, and a bright spot in the day-just being there-are all documented benefits.

Studies show that pet visits provide warmth and affection for everyone involved. Laughter, recollection of pleasant memories, mental stimulation for Alzheimer's patients, reduction in blood pressure, distraction from depression, reduction in incidence of heart attacks, increase in incidence of survival and speed of recovery from heart attacks, are among the areas animals are being used effectively

Animals aid in relaxation and decrease anxiety. Petting an animal is a rhythmic, repetitive activity which can act as a passive meditative focus. Interacting with an animal has been shown to reduce the cardiovascular, behavioral, and psychological indicators of stress. For example, watching fish in an aquarium was found to be as effective as hypnosis in reducing anxiety in patients awaiting dental surgery.

Astonishingly, animal therapy has been recorded since the 9th Century when doctors in Flanders encouraged disabled patients to look after animals to "re-establish the harmony of soul and body." Psychiatrists and psychologists in formal psychotherapy have also used animals for many years. This was probably a natural outgrowth of pet owners typically talking informally to their animals as if they were human.

Play is an essential feature of social, intellectual, physical and emotional growth for children. It is also an important ingredient in animal therapy. Pets are nonjudgmental playmates that will provide play on demand, are always willing to chase a ball, go for a walk, or interact with us.

Children are shown to be able to better deal with traumatic experiences if they own an animal. Animals have helped to rouse youngsters from a coma and are at times taken into the intensive care unit to assist with recovery.

Children learn empathy, how to care for others, how to build self-confidence, and take responsibility through feeding, training and exercising their pet. Today, the exercise they get is of equal importance.

People who own pets report better health when compared to non-pet owners, and it has been shown that pet owners on Medicaid make fewer visits to their doctors than non-owners.

Interpersonal communication, one of the biggest needs, particularly with the aged, is among the animal specialties. Multiple studies have shown that the presence of an animal leads to the interpretation of social scenes as less threatening and improves perceived character.

Animals promote people interplay. They have often been termed "social lubricants" as a result of facilitating these social interactions. They are a conversation piece and a safe topic between people. Something as simple as walking a dog through a park was found beneficial in a study conducted by Peter Messent of the Animal Studies Center in London. He found that people walking in the park with a dog engaged in more social activity than when they walked alone.

More than one scientific study using healthy adults, healthy children, and adults with high blood pressure, has confirmed that simply being in the presence of a dog, or petting an animal can reduce blood pressure.

Another program, The Eden Alternative, uses animals that were rescued at animal shelters to assist with their extensive programs in nursing homes. Not only has patient health improved as a result of creating companion relationships with the animals, but the spiraling effect of doubling visitation after animal involvement has had a further positive effect. Richmond, Virginia SPCA is building a similar program, to be the first in the southeast. Across the nation many projects of this nature are under way.

Two other studies have shown that owning a dog had a significant effect on survival after a heart attack. Patients who were admitted to the hospital with a heart attack were followed for one year. The researchers found that patients who were alive one year after leaving the hospital were more likely to own a pet.

The Shiloh Project in Fairfax, Virginia works both ways. They team up an "at risk" child with a "homeless" dog. These children have a history of violence or abuse towards animals or people, or are victims of abuse and violence. The child is paired with another child and a homeless dog three times a week at school. They spend time learning how to train a dog, and undergo humane education and communication exercises. This program has been helping children break their cycle of violence while transforming an unwanted dog into an animal that is adopted into a loving family.

Horses are proving to be particularly effective in the treatment of addictive behavior. "Equine-facilitated therapy" originated in 1991 at Arizona's Sierra Tucson Center. The guide Horse Foundation in Kittrell, North Carolina, near Raleigh, is training seeing-eye equines to compete with the long established dog supplying the eyes for the blind. These miniature horses can live 30 to 40 years, far longer than dogs, and have a wide field of vision from their two side-mounted eyes, making them perfect candidates for service to the sightless.

The value of animals in promoting healing and growth is becoming increasingly recognized among professional care providers, clinical practitioners, and educators. Today, trained and certified animal/handler teams are used in medical, psychiatric, rehabilitation, and special education facilities throughout the world to provide a medium for assisting individuals where traditional methods fall short.

In many hospitals animals are as much a part of the ward routine as doctor rounds, pill distribution, and meal trolleys. It's not unusual to see dogs, cats, rabbits, and guinea pigs on the team.

Something as simple as swimming with dolphins or riding a horse can pay big dividends. Be on the lookout for those shingles. Don't be surprised if one day you encounter an animal's name on one. It might require the redesign of the stethoscope but it could be the next breakthrough in medicine.

Medicine like so many other professions has gone through several experimental stages in an effort to make our lives more comfortable. The following discussion reviews animal's role in the trials.

It's never fun to be sick. When we feel poorly or have pain, we want relief. When experiencing discomfort, most of us start with a home remedy, perhaps something that has been handed down from grandparents or something we read in a book. The next move for assistance may be to the drug store. If the illness persists, off to the doctor we go.

Before taking that last step you may wish to try some of the treatments attributed to our animal friends. Animals have been practicing medicine by way of superstition, myth, or just plain faith for a long time. Without benefit of printed text, computers or formal schooling, the animal kingdom is reported to have contributed to the healing of man. Lacking stethoscope, modern medical advances or machinery, creatures have managed to appear in many curative suggestions passed down from various periods in our history

The recommendations below include a variety of animal involvement for interesting approaches for curing ailments for every thing from the common cold all the way to rheumatism. It seems like it would be easy to recover with the number of choices offered, however ridiculous some may appear. We must also remember that medicine is a science and these corrective measures are not always founded on fact.

A special warning to children; before you use any of these procedures check with your parents, they are mostly for fun, and could be very dangerous if misused. Whatever the selected treatment don't use the forefinger of the right hand to put on medicine or the sore will never heal. That is the finger witches point with while putting evil spells on their victims.

Cow manure is recommended as a good cure for aches and pains. Not much more attractive is the suggestion to cure asthma. Sticking the tanned skin of a mole to the patient's chest with honey is the suggestion for its cure. Perhaps more attractive is the suggestion of sleeping on a bear skin to cure a back ache.

Some men are troubled by baldness others think it appealing. Badger oil could be the answer for both. It is said to be a cure for baldness and equally effective for thinning hair. This hard to acquire substance is also popular when put in medicinal concoctions for such diverse ailments as coughs, rheumatism, and sprained ankles.

According to American Indian traditional belief, rubbing the head with mackerel flies is another way to care for the problem.

Placing a necklace made from a string dropped in mole's blood around a child's neck is said to prevent bed-wetting but it might be difficult to get the child to agree to such treatment.

You also might think twice (or more) before duplicating the practice of the Cherokee Indians to keep away contagious diseases. They believed that the scent of the skunk did the trick. They hung a "scent bag" over the doorway and pierced a small hole through the bag so the scent would permeate the room.

Colds are the least dangerous of our ills, but can be very annoying, particularly when accompanied by a fever. Some people believe the grease of bear brains protects us from colds, and alleviates the aches in our muscles, as well as reducing swollen joints. Others regard goose grease rubbed on the chest as an effective medication for colds.

For the fever, bed bugs taken internally in powder form are supposed to take care of lowering it. Feathers of a black hen burned under your bed will also work well. In certain areas of Ohio a mixture of bed bugs and beans is accepted as a cure for both chill and fever.

If your cold includes an ear ache, as they often do, you may have to intensify the medication. Take a wood-boring beetle and cut off its head, allow one drop to flow in your ear. If you find it easier to find the fat of a fox, warm that and place it in the ear for the same result. Tea made from the dried droppings of a wild male rabbit will cure fever when consumed every half-hour until sweating starts.

Colds that come with a sore throat require more drastic measures; roast, mince, and then eat a mouse to get relief.

Various cultures use the lady bug for cures, including remedies for colic and measles.

For the drunkard, put eggs of an owl or a live eel in the drunken man's drink. A sobering thought.

Moose hooves were at one time used to cure hundreds of afflictions. The left hind foot, for example, was used as a cure for epilepsy. Rings made from the antlers were used to cure headaches and dizziness. Mixed with various herbs, they were used as an antidote for snakebite.

Many folks think that freckles are attractive while others are not so fond of them. If you are a member of the latter group the way to get rid of them is go to a brook, catch a frog and rub him alive over your face. Or you may decide freckles aren't so bad after all.

Headaches trouble a great number but they are easy to fix; just bind the head of a buzzard around the forehead.

Deer antlers mixed with herbs were thought to cure impotency. A young buck, boiled in its velvet (the soft skin on the antlers), has been used to treat dropsy.

Jaundice can be cured by rolling a live spider in a little butter and swallowing it. The bone in the fog fish's head will help cure kidney stones.

For lameness try skunk grease or wild cat grease. Just as beaver fat is believed to be effective in calming nerves, the above lubricants are held to nurture bones. If it's just leg cramps that bother you, soothe them by wearing an eel skin or a mole skin around the leg.

Rheumatism can be very painful but our animal friends offer a choice of cure for this dreaded ailment. Inducing bees to sting the affected area, wearing an eel skin around the waist, or carrying a haddock bone, all enjoy a good reputation for relief. A hare's right forefoot or ashes of a turtle shell are said to have the same value.

The number of treatments for rheumatism might also be effective for preventing worry if you decide to forgo the beaver fat remedy to calm your nerves. If shyness is your problem wearing a fox's tongue as an amulet will help.

To cure Scarlet fever, cut some hair from the patient's head and stuff it down the throat of a donkey.

Sprains and bruises can be handled using raccoon fat as a rub and sometimes as a substitute for lard. For stomach pains tying a cormorant skin around your abdomen will give comfort. If the pain is severe, cobra venom has been found to be useful in giving relief.

If Toothaches are the problem carry the forelegs and one hind leg from a mole in your pocket. Another approach says a rat's tail, dried and powdered, will stop it from hurting. As last resort take one or two ladybugs, smash them, and stuff them into the cavity of the tooth.

Dog's fat is a charm against tuberculosis. It can also be cured by swallowing baby frogs before breakfast. Ground-elk hoof has long been used in folk medicine as a cure for vertigo.

If it's warts that are bothering you, take care of them by killing a cat and burying it in a black stocking or rub them with a peeled apple and then give the apple to a pig. As a last resort drink blood from a hedgehog.

Mice have been useful in curing whooping cough, fevers, chills, toothaches, and stammering. Tea made from white ants has also proved to be an effective therapeutic for whooping cough.

Such choices! It appears there will have to be some refinements before animals take over the medical profession.

Animals used in cures above.
Ants
Beaver
Bed bugs
Bees
Buzzard
Cats
Deer
Dog

Dolphin
Donkey
Eels
Elk
Fish
Fox
Frog
Goose
Guinea Pig
Hare
Horse
Lady bug
Mackerel flies
Mice
Mole
Moose
Pig
Rabbit
Skunk
Snake
Spider

Law Enforcement/Fire Departments/Military

Law enforcement agencies have used dogs to assist their investigations for many years. Their incredibly sensitive noses, several thousand times better than humans, is a real asset in sniffing out tiny quantities of substances. They can distinguish particular scents with amazing accuracy. With special training they are most effective in detecting illegal substance for local police, the FBI, and custom officers.

The successful use of dogs by military units during World War 1 brought added attention to the use of dogs in police work-see below. The most popular breeds for these activities are German Shepherds, Golden Retrievers, and Labrador Retrievers. Many of the dogs used are rescued from dog pounds and animal shelters or donated by owners.

Since the nineteenth-century dogs have accompanied policemen on their patrol of the streets. The use of canines in America is a relatively recent pursuit. The United States Police Canine Association (USPCA) wasn't founded until 1971, when programs were developed to establish minimum standards for the training of police dogs.

No denying police work is very dangerous for the dogs. Many have died on duty. In several jurisdictions the intentional injuring or killing of a police dog is a felony, carrying harsher penalties than those in the statues embodied in local animal cruelty laws, just as an assault on a police officer is often a more serious offense that the same assault on a non-officer. A police dog killed in the line of duty is often given a full-police funeral.

Pennies to Protect Police Dogs, Inc, a program started by a 12-year old Florida girl and administered by USPCA, raised more than $225,000 to provide custom-fit bulletproof and stab-resistant vests for police dogs employed at 145 agencies in twenty-seven states.

Dogs are also effective in searching buildings and other areas for suspects and evidence, tracking criminals and lost people, pursuing and apprehending fleeing criminals, and protecting their human handlers. Among the noteworthy tasks they have performed includes using them for intimidation purposes during the civil rights protests of the 1960s.

Dogs have also been successful working with federal agencies that guard the borders. Sniffing out narcotics being smuggled into the country at major border crossings has reduced this activity. The Animal Plant Health Inspection Service uses dogs to sniff out people's luggage for banned plant and animal products at major airports. People sometimes try to sneak in items that could pose a disease threat to America's crops and animals.

Much of the above activity was grouped into the Department of Homeland Security in 2003. The canine resources of the individual agencies were combined into a new agency called U.S. Customs and Border Protection (CBP). Over 1,000 canine teams in operation are stationed at airports, seaports, and border crossings around the country.

The department outlines their objectives and purpose as follows:

To unite in a common cause all law enforcement agencies utilizing the services of the canine as an aid in the prevention and detection of crime.

To promote friendship and brotherhood between all those interested in the training and utilization of the canine in police work.

To endeavor to establish a minimum working standard, and improve the abilities of the canine in police work, thereby rendering better service to the community.

To establish and maintain a legal assistance fund for acts resulting in civil suits from the use of police trained canines.

To coordinate the exchange of any advanced techniques of training of the utilization of police dogs.

To improve the image of the working police dog to the populace in general through improved public service in the prevention and detection of crime.

To aid and assist those law enforcement agencies making application for information concerning the establishment of canine sections within their respective departments.

The federal government started a breeding program to develop Labrador retrievers specifically for detective work. Puppies are kept in a breeding facility until they are twelve weeks old and then raised by foster families until they are about a year old. Officials report dogs have discovered millions of pounds of marijuana, cocaine, heroin, and other drugs hidden in vehicles and cargo entering the United States. During 2001 they led customs agents to more than one million pounds of marijuana and 26,000 pounds of cocaine, resulting in the arrest of nearly 8,000 people. More than $20 million in cash was also confiscated.

As in any team, stars surface. In 2003, a CBP dog named Crazy Joe was credited with uncovering more than $10 million in illegal drugs at the John F. Kennedy Airport in New York City. We could nominate this superstar for the "Heistman Award." Drug sniffing dogs are also sometimes used in schools.

We can't forget horses have also been used by law enforcement for centuries. As the fastest and surest form of transportation for officers for many years they continued to be used for mounted patrols, even after cars became common, in hundreds of jurisdictions around the United States and elsewhere. Canada's mounted police are probably the best known.

Mounted units are popular in both rural and metropolitan areas. They are particularly useful in backcountry areas on dirt roads and rugged terrain. Several U. S. police departments use horses for crowd control during strikes, rallies, parades, athletic events, concerts, and other public demonstrations. They are also used to provide greater visibility of officers on the streets.

The use of horses to contain crowds is not always popular. During protests horses and the riders are exposed to people who may be angry and confrontational. There are reports of police horses being pelted with marbles and even garbage. Protesters claim that police often charge their horses into crowds, knocking over and injuring people.

Just as with the dogs this can be dangerous work for the horses. Walking for many hours on city streets under stressful conditions is not easy on them. A few instances are reported each year of police horses throwing off or kicking their riders.

Fire Departments

Many fire departments use dogs as part of their arson investigation teams. Arson dogs are special-trained to sniff for the presence of accelerants, such as gasoline, at sites where arson is suspected. Once again, their incredible sense of smell can detect tiny amounts of accelerants lingering on surfaces inside buildings and vehicles or on people's clothes. The training includes teaching the dog to indicate a find either by sitting or attempting to gain eye contact with their handlers so as to not arouse suspicion, because arsonists often hang around the scene of the crime. The next step is to discreetly lead the dog through the crowd gathered to sniff the presence of accelerants on people's clothing or belongings.

Animals in the Military

Military units around the world have long-recognized the intelligence of animals to assist in their assignments. A variety of animals have played important functions; dogs, pigs, oxen, camels, horses, elephants, pigeons, dolphins, rats, dwarf orcas, sea lions among them. From spying cats to bomb-sniffing bees, animals have served some bizarre roles in military operations. Some are recognized below.

Dogs have served the military in many capacities. They are used as sentries, to smell out explosives, land mines, booby traps, snipers, and even as anti-tank weapons with explosives attached to their back. Dogs don't necessarily compete with pigeons as messenger but are used in appropriate circumstances. They are utilized to scare horses and pounce on their dislodged enemy mounts. The popularity of the K 9 corps helped to gain dogs the recognition they deserve for their outstanding contribution to soldiers around the world. Thousands have served with distinction.

Pigeons served many purposes during the war, racing through the skies with airplanes, serving as a guide for missiles or even being fitted with cameras to take pictures of enemy positions. But one of the most important roles they served was as messengers.

When the United States entered World War I in 1917, the Army Signal Corps was given 600 pigeons for the purpose of passing messages when it couldn't be done by signal flag or field phone. The pigeons were donated by bird breeders in Great Britain, and then trained for their jobs by American soldiers. The army had an entire Pigeon Breeding and Training Center at Fort Monmouth, NJ where the pigeons were trained to carry small capsules containing messages, maps, photographs and cameras.

It was an important job but very dangerous. If the enemy soldiers were nearby when a pigeon was released, they knew that the bird would be carrying important messages, and tried their best to shoot the pigeon down so the message couldn't be delivered. Military historians claim that more than ninety percent of all pigeon-carried messages sent by the U.S. Army during the war were received.

Probably the most famous of all the carrier pigeons was one named *Cher Ami,* two French words meaning "Dear Friend". Cher Ami served several months on the front lines during the fall of 1918. He flew 12 important missions to deliver messages. Perhaps the most important was the message he carried on October 4, 1918. The story is told in Harry Webb Farrington's poem.

Cher Ami

Cher Ami how do you do
Listen, let me talk to you
I'll not hurt you, don't you see
Come a little close to me

Little scrawny blue and white
Messenger for men who fight
Tell me of the deep, red scar
There where just no feathers are

What about your poor left leg
Tell me Cher Ami, I beg
Boys and girls are at a loss.
How you won that Silver Cross
The finest fun that came to me
Was when I went with Whittlesey
We marched so fast, so far ahead
We are all lost,' the keeper said
"Mon Cher Ame-that's my dear friend
You are the one we'll have to send
The whole battalion is lost
And you must win at any cost.
So with the message tied on tight
I flew up straight with all my might
Before I got up high enough,
Those watchful guns began to puff

Machine-gun bullets came like rain
You'd think I was an aeroplane
And when I started to the rear
My! The shots were coming near.
But on I flew, straight as a bee
The wind could not catch up with me
Until I dropped out of the air
Into our own men's camp, so there!"
But Cher Ami, upon my word
You modes, modest little bird
Now don't you know that you forgot
Tell us how your leg and breast were shot
Oh yes, the day we crossed the Meuse
I flew to Rampont with the news
Again the bullets came like hail
I thought for sure that I should fail,
The bullets buzzed by like a bee
So close, it almost frightened me
One struck the feathers of this sail
Another went right through my tail
But when I got back to the rear
I found they hit me, her and here
But that's nothing never mind
I only care for what they said,
For when they saw the way I bled,
And found in front a swollen lump,
The message hanging from this stump
The French and Mine said, 'Tres bien'
Or 'Very good-American
'Mon Cher Ami, you brought good news
Our army's gone across the Meuse
You surely had a lucky call
And I'm so glad I guess that's all
I'll sit, so pardon me, I beg
It's hard a-standing on one let

Today, visitors to the National Museum of American History, Smithsonian Institution, Washington, D.C. can still see Cher Ami, preserved for history alongside the French Croix de Guerre with palm that was awarded to him by the French government. Cher Ami died of his multiple war wounds on June 13, 1919-less than a year after completing this heroic flight.

The K-9 corp has its share of exceptional stories as well. One of particular interest involves a dog "Spike" and a marine Jared Heine. They served in more than 100 combat missions patrolling for explosive devises in the Helmand providence of Afghanistan.

Heine was injured on three occasions by explosions and returned to the United States suffering from memory loss and post-traumatic stress disorder. Not knowing if he would ever see Spike again added to his discomfort.

Heine's mother learned the dog had been assigned to work with the Capitol police in DC. Laura Taylor of that agency had worked with Spike in more than 800 sweeps following 870 hours training. Despite her attachment she answered the call for reuniting Spike with his battle partner. The love and commitment these two shared and the enormous responsibility they shouldered in such a dangerous environment made for an emotional regret allowing the dog to rejoin his fellow marine but Taylor agreed, it was the right thing to do..

Now Spike is in his third assignment as a "healer" assisting Heine in his recovery. That should be easier than searching for mines and bomb sniffing.

The horse has a long military history dating back to pulling chariots of early warriors and equipment. They continue to be effective in transferring troops, ammunition and gear; especially over difficult terrain. Mules were similarly used and often able to maneuver terrain not agreeable to horses. Camels were employed in arid areas and when the territory was sandy.

War horses were also trained to bite and kick. The invention of the stirrup contributed to the horse-mounted cavalry becoming the most prestigious military unit for centuries, The Lipizzan were particularly good at these maneuvers and valuable for surveillance.

It is appropriate to note that so many of the heroes honored with statues throughout the world are depicted on their mounts. Recognition for contribution of the horse alone has not been overlooked entirely. Statues throughout the world give credence to their service.

In Virginia two tributes stand out. Andrew Mellon conscience of so many statues honoring individuals and regiments participating in the Civil War but none for animals, commissioned an honor to be placed at the Virginia Historical

Society. The statue was done by Teresa Pulliam, an internationally known sculptor, noted for her work in horses. She also did the Mellon Kentucky Derby winner Sea Hero. Two smaller copies of the horse are found at the National Sporting Museum in Middleburg, Virginia and at the United States Cavalry Museum in Fort Riley, Kansas. The message that accompanies the monument reads as follows.

IN MEMORY
OF THE ONE AND ONE HALF MILLION
HORSES AND MULES OF THE CONFEDERATE
AND UNION ARMIES WHO WERE KILLED,
WERE WOUNDED OR DIED FROM DISEASE
IN THE CIVIL WAR

A Korean War hero horse, winner of two Purple Hearts, is memorialized at the Marine Corp Museum in Quantico, Virginia.

Dolphins have been serving in the U.S. Navy for more than 40 years as part of the Navy's Marine Mammal Program, and they were used during the Vietnam War and Operation Iraqi Freedom. These highly intelligent animals are trained to detect, locate and mark mines, and in object recovery in the sea.

When they detect an intruder the dolphin touches a sensor on a boat to alert its handler, and the handler then places a strobe light or noisemaker on the dolphin's nose. The dolphin is trained to swim to the intruder, bump him or her from behind to knock the device off its nose and swim away while military personnel take over.

Trained sea lions, part of the same program, locate and tag mines just like dolphins, but that's not all these "Navy Seals" do-they also cuff underwater intruders. The sea lions carry a spring clamp in their mouths that can be attached to a swimmer or diver by simply pressing it against the person's leg. In fact, the sea lions are so fast that the clamp is on before the swimmer is even aware of it. Once a person is clamped, sailors aboard ships can pull the swimmer out of the water by the rope attached to the clamp. These specially trained sea lions, part of the Navy's Shallow Water Intruder Detection System, patrol Navy bases and were even deployed to protect ships from terrorists in the Persian Gulf.

Perhaps not as well-known for service, the elephant has been a long time war participant. They were effective as mounts and for moving heavy loads especially for Hannibal during the Second Punic War. Elephant's main use has been to charge the enemy trampling them and breaking their ranks and instilling terror. They performed well in World War 11 penetrating areas where vehicles couldn't break through.

Oxen have also been used to transport heavy equipment and are numbered among a pantheon of others, pigs, horses, dogs and camels that have taken on loads and served by detecting bomb danger.

Honeybees are natural-born sniffers with antennae able to sense pollen in the wind and track it down to specific flowers, so bees are now being trained to recognize the scents of bomb ingredients. When the bees pick up a suspicious odor with their antennae, they flick their proboscises-a tubular feeding organ-that extends from their mouths.

In practice, a honeybee bomb-detection unit would look like a simple box stationed outside airport security or a train platform. Inside the box, bees would be strapped into tubes and exposed to puffs of air where they could constantly check for the faint scent of a bomb. A video camera linked to pattern-recognition software would alert authorities when the bees started waving their proboscises in unison.

Insect cyborgs in the military might sound like something out of a science-fiction movie, but the U.S Department of Defense is developing such creatures as part of its Hybrid Insect Initiative. Scientists implant electronic controls into insect's bodies during the early stages of metamorphosis and allow tissue to grow around them. The insects can then be tracked, controlled and used to gather or transmit information. For example, a caterpillar could carry a microphone to record conversations or a gas sensor to detect a chemical attack.

Even bears have aided the military. One popular story of Voytek, a baby brown bear, found wandering the hills of Iran in 1943, by the Second Polish Transport Company, makes the point. The soldiers took him in, feeding him condensed milk, and before long he became a part of the unit-even enjoying beers and cigarettes with his fellow soldiers.

As Voytek grew into a 6-foot, 250-pound bear, he was trained to carry mortar shells and boxes of ammunition during battle, and in 1944 he was officially enlisted in the Polish Army;-complete with name, rank and number. The bear traveled with his unit, carried ammunition to soldiers under fire and once even discovered an Arab spy hiding in the unit's bath hut. After the war, the Edinburgh Zoo became Voytek's new home and he lived there until his death in 1963.

Not all animal military service has been successful. During the Cold War, the CIA attempted to transform an ordinary domestic cat into a sophisticated bugging device as part of Operation Acoustic Kitty. The idea was to surgically alter cats so they could eavesdrop on Soviet conversations from park benches and windowsills.

The project began in 1961 when the CIA implanted a battery and a microphone into a cat and turned its tail into an antenna. But the cat wandered off when it was hungry, a problem that had to be addressed in another operation. Finally, after five years, several surgeries, intensive training and $15 million, the cat was ready for its first field test.

The CIA drove the cat to a Soviet compound on Wisconsin Avenue in Washington, D.C. and let it out of a parked van across the street. The cat walked into the road and was immediately hit by a taxi. Operation Acoustic Kitty was declared a failure and completely abandoned in 1967.

Toward the end of World War II, the Air Force was looking for a more effective way to attack Japanese cities when Dr. Lytle S. Adams, a dental surgeon, contacted the White House with an idea. Adams suggested strapping small incendiary devices to bats, loading them into cages shaped like bombshells and dropping them from a plane. Bats would then escape from the shells and find their way into factories and other buildings where they would rest until their miniature bombs exploded.

The U.S. military began developing these "bat bombs" in the early 1940s, but the first test went awry when the bats set fire to an Air Force base in Carlsbad, New Mexico. After that, the project was turned over to the Navy, which completed a successful concept where the bats were released over a mock-up of a Japanese city. More tests were scheduled for the summer of 1944, but the program was canceled because of its slow progress. The U.S. military invested an estimated $2 million in the project.

Armor & Weapons

More than one idea for weaponry came from observation of animal's sharp teeth, claws, fangs, hooves, use of poison stingers and darts, and other projectiles. Could the dragon have been responsible for the development of the flame thrower?

Military armor was no doubt influenced by observing animal's bearers of protection such as hermit crabs, crocodiles, lobsters, oysters, crabs, snails, turtles and armadillos. The Exoskeletons of spiders and insects surely had an impact as well.

Animals have used a variety of approaches to evade predators by looking and behaving like something else, playing dead, changing color to blend with the terrain, or making themselves appear bigger and as a last resort stand up and fight. When reviewing the methods of camouflage used by animals it is easy to see how the military benefited from observing the techniques of those gifted in the art of invisibility to design their own camouflage tactics.

Animals are experts at camouflage. They use it in many forms for protection from their enemies and for hunting. Being able to blend with the background is an asset. Whether mud, grass, gravel, flower or water most animals have learned one or more methods by changing color, counter shadowing patterns, and mimicking to deceive their predator or prey.

Chameleons and cuttle-fish are two examples of having the ability to change colors anytime in quick fashion. Ptarmigan, stoats, weasels, deer and artic fox do it over a longer period to coincide with the terrain during the changing seasons.

Animals have shown us other effective forms of protection. Skunks store a very unpleasant liquid in their anal glands. Animals like lizards and toads make themselves bigger. Hedgehogs and porcupines roll into a ball to take advantage of their spiny outside, opossums take a different tact by playing dead.

Turtles carry their protection with them in the form of a shell and the hermit crab has learned to use a neighbor's house for protection. Underground passage is another ploy used by many animals like prairie dogs and rabbits, not to mention the beaver.

Rhinoceros make use of the big horn they carry and deer, elk and moose are more than qualified to use their antlers. Stings and venom are other forms of protection. Bees, wasps, tarantulas, spiders and some ants and even ticks can get your attention with a bite. Snakes can get a grip on a problem and when necessary inject poisonous venom. That is really effective as is the anal acid the wood ant sprays.

Group defense may not be considered a form of camouflage but it is an effective defense mechanism. The musk ox is noted for this approach. They form a circle facing outward with their young inside the ring for protection.

Construction

We build our homes from a great number of materials. Early man began with the earthy sod and mud. After graduating to wood, stone, brick, and metal he then moved to sophisticated plastics, tiles, glass, and high tempered steel. Nails, screws, cement, tape, and tar help us to keep our abodes intact. Where do you think the ideas originated?

Animals were the original craftsmen. A million and a half different animals live on the earth, and must create dwellings for themselves. Whether a new design or adapting an existing home of another specie, animals are proven master builders.

Their building materials consist of trees, shrubs, roots, sticks, bark, rocks, shells, feathers, fur, seeds, grasses, ferns, and plants. They are not opposed to decorating with bottle tops, metal buttons, nails, silverware, keys, hair curlers, paper, and other human detritus. Saliva, sap, resin, wax, silk, mosses, mud, waste, soil, and water are all used as mortar in their habitat. Some animals even manufacture special substances within their bodies for this purpose.

Adding color to their creations they use Mother Nature herself without a trip to the paint store. Their pallet includes berries, withered flowers, lichen, mosses, algae, seaweed, stones, roots, and odds and ends found in nature, and the scrap piles of human projects.

Without benefit of man's technological advances animals have been experts in structural engineering for eons. They accomplish this by using their beaks, mouths, claws, needles, antenna, horns, teeth, feet, and noses. Animals never packaged their originality as a Swiss-knife or power tools but many were instrumental in the development of man's basic tools.

After selecting a site animals have to be aware of a proper spot for protection from predators. They take into consideration a multitude of other factors: total space, camouflage, accessibility, exposure to wind and rain, gradients of light, temperature, humidly, and odors; each of which must be weighed against the others. Their designs are organized to maximize comfort while raising a family. Evidence of their ingenuity can be found underground, in the depths of the ocean, and in the treetops of mountains. Tunnels, toilet areas, food storage sections, trap doors, chimneys, nurseries, and escape routes are commonplace in their structures. Animals design techniques were first to perfect the use of insulation, ventilation, air conditioning, and drainage.

For a look on the light-side think of the Flintstones who are noted for their imaginative use of animals to assist in everyday chores. Wilma did the dishes with the help of an octopus, birds were her crocheting needles, she used a mastodon as a vacuum, and she pressed her clothes using a turtle as an iron.

Besides making a living driving his dinosaur crane, Fred employed the creature as an elevator lift and as a draw bridge. He shaved using a bumblebee as a razor, birds were his hedge clippers, and a crab his lawn mower. He used a turtle as a car jack and a bird doubled as the horn for his car.

A mastodon served as the Flintstone's mammoth shower and the porcupine was used as a scrub brush. Their toaster was a dragon, a pelican served as a trash can and a mail box, birds were utilized as alarm clocks, clothes pins, letter openers and as a sewing machine.

These are fun things but were based on the contribution animals made to the tools used by modern man. Some tools have even retained the animal's name (monkey wrench, grub hoe, dovetail plane) in recognition of their development after observing a member of the animal kingdom accomplishing the task which the tool performs.

Not all the tools using animal names are well-known. The rat and the pig are two good examples. The RAT, or Rock Abrasion Tool, is on a robotic arm of the rover that landed on Mars. The RAT grinds off the surface of rocks so that scientists can examine what's inside them. The PIG is used to clean the inside of a pipe; a SNAKE performs the same function in the home to clear clogged toilets and drains. Probably the biggest pig (maybe a hog?) is used to clean Alaska's Pipeline that brings oil from Prudhoe Bay.

Man living in simple apartments, houses, or luxurious mansions, whether built in clusters or in isolation, has been unable to compete with animal engineers when it comes to perfectly suiting the dwelling to the resident. Despite tools of all descriptions he has had little success improving animal techniques. The creature construction masters have taught us a lot.

The listing below gives credence to other animal innovations adapted by man. It is fun to speculate how such a variety of tools and products may have come about because of an animal trailblazer. Some may exaggerate the kingdoms role but all are worth a consideration. Try to add to the list.

With a little imagination one could think both the aardvark and anteater had something to do with the making of the straw. The alligator's long toothed jaw influenced clips to hold things together and its serrated jaws the same for gripping irregular shaped parts and development of pinking shears. Who could deny antlers were the first hat racks or the observation that beavers gave the idea for goggles.

Watching a bird scurry the ground was probably responsible for the first hand cultivator. The caterpillar gave the idea for tractors and tanks. Moles could have had something to do with the development of the plow. No doubt ladders came from observing giraffes dining on Acadia trees and goats were instrumental for the idea of our trash demolition machinery. Who is to say that the first fly swatters weren't influenced by elephants that use plants to combat their nuisance?

Hares were a natural showing the way for snow shoes as the hummingbird was for designing the helicopter. The barn owl was the first satellite dish and marsupials had the first baby carriers. Was it the pig or porcupine that gave man the idea for brush bristles? It's a good bet snakes could claim the idea for pliers and the vise. Squirrels might be credited with influencing storage tanks and perhaps the umbrella. It's conceivable turtles were the fore runners of motor homes and campers.

The structural lessons of the beaver, probably the most respected builder in the kingdom, are far-reaching. Their instruction, from acquiring the material to the final product in a difficult environment, has been an inspiration to many. Considering the beaver is surrounded with myths, we end with a review of several of these beliefs which may suggest we should investigate the information we get regardless the source.

1. The belief beavers carry cargoes of mud on their tails while swimming is false. They do transport quantities of mud and sticks, but by holding the material in their forepaws against their bodies, but nothing would ride very long on a swimming beaver's tail-least of all mud. This incidentally debunks the notion that beavers use their tails as trowels in mixing up the "mud mortar" used in building their houses and dams. Rather, they use their mouths and forepaws in their construction projects, the tail for help in swimming and, some suggest, to sound an alarm by slapping down on the water.

2. The thought that beavers can fell a tree wherever they want to is exaggerated. In fact, wherever beaver have cut trees, one sees many that fell the wrong way and were abandoned. Occasionally beavers are killed by trees they themselves cut down.

3. .The notion that beavers only cut small to medium-sized trees, usually poplar needs reexamining. They prefer poplar for food, but will cut down trees at least eighteen inches in diameter of hard woods like beech, cherry, and even oak.

4 That dams constructed by beavers always has a curvature that withstands the thrust of the head of water. Sometimes beaver dams do embody this curvature, but there are many dams that are zigzag and of various patterns. There seems to be no consistency of design.

5. The claim there was a decimation of the beaver in the nineteenth century and the beaver trade became nonexistent is a stretch. It is true that the beaver was slaughtered indiscriminately during the height of the fashion: the fashion, by the way, being men's beaver hats, not woman's fur coats. That the fashion is very old is indicated in the Prologue to Geoffrey Chaucer's Canterbury Tales, written in the 1380s; Chaucer describes a prosperous merchant as wearing "Upon his heed a Flaundrysh (Flemish) beaver hat."

Beaver hats continued to be popular in Europe until the mid-nineteenth century, when the beaver supply waned and silk became popular instead is suspect. Beaver hair is particularly well adapted to making felt; vast quantities of it were used for this purpose.

Hundreds of thousands of beavers were slain each year between 1800 and 1850. By 1900 the catch had fallen off drastically. Now the beaver has come back, and the annual take is as great as it was during the height of the fur trade in the nineteenth century.

Communicating with Animal Language

Animals frequently appear in our definitions, expressions, clichés, quotations, and proverbs. They emerge from our lexicon to communicate metaphorically in our conversations and literature. The amusing story below attempts to highlight a number of these references. An effort to report on the animals in alphabetical order comes close.

When a friend is burdened we may refer to them having an "albatross around their neck." When leaving a meeting or a visit it is common to say, "See you later alligator." If the departure is hurried it may be because one of the parties "had ants in their pants."

Being subject to a rule one doesn't agree with is often referred to by declaring "the law is an ass." Silly rules can "badger" you especially when the rule is "blind as a bat." Lawyers are sometimes "loaded for bear" when they try to defend the ridiculous. It's a "beastly task" and can keep one "busy as a beaver' 'making a "beeline" to the courthouse."

In all endeavors remember it is the "early bird that gets the worm." Most "young bucks" are slow to learn this and get "buffaloed" before they catch on to "grab the bull by the horns." Some "dumb bunnies" never get it until they are "old buzzards." They act like a "canary that just swallowed the cat" when they finally catch on. They should have paid more attention when they were "spring chickens" but they were so "cock-sure of themselves" they didn't pay the price.

"Holy cow" it takes some "old coots" a long time to avoid going "cuckoo" instead of jumping in to learn. It may not be "cricket" but all they want to do is "crab." No one is going to shed "crocodile tears"" for them, let them "eat crow."

"Running like a deer" from responsibility is the route to ending up as "dog meat." Some won't learn in "donkey years," they let education "roll off like "water off a ducks back." This lack of initiative really "ruffles your feathers."

Most have a "memory like an elephant" but their effort is "slippery as an eel." They "fish for compliments" and time flies by while they "flounder around" outwardly acting "sly as a fox" while carrying "a frog in their throat" from anxiety.

"Take a gander" as they try to avoid being "a scrape goat" knowing full well their "goose is cooked." They'll end up being "gophers" and be "knee high in grasshoppers" before amounting to anything. Individuals like this end up being "guinea pigs" and pay a big price for their "harebrained' 'gullible sloth."

Some may live "high on the hog" but chances are most will be "hen-pecked" at home and always "stirring up a hornet's nest" at the office. They may think the can get by "horsing around" but the odds are rather than "hunting with the hounds" they will end up being "jackasses."

Any good businessman would tell them to go fly a kite. That may make them "nervous as a kitten" but they should get used to such "lamb basting." To be "happy as a lark" one must get the "lion's share" of good luck

"Holy mackerel", I don't mean to "make a mountain of a mole hill" but one that keeps "monkeying around,' 'quiet as a mouse" and "stubborn as a mule" is not what I would call "wise as a owl." One must know when their "ox is being gored" and make changes.

If you want the "world to be your oyster," stop "strutting like a peacock," take off that "penguin suit," give up the "pig headed" attitude and forget "partying with the animals."

If you think life is a game of "playing possum" you are a "pigeon." Attitudes like that "multiply like rabbits." It's time to "pony up" get "off that rail fence,' 'ram in some real effort" and "join the rat race."

Round off those "scalloped edges" and seal off your destiny to be "like a can of sardines" like all the "sharks of life." Why be like the "black sheep" of society. The days of being "a shrimp" and "drinking like a fish" until you are "drunk as a skunk" are over.

Change your slug from one of drink to one of coin; to invest in your future. Swallow your pride, get off the "snail's pace" and start "squirreling away" for the future. This can be your "swan song"-the pace can be swift changing you from a "turkey" to a "tiger." You have "weaseled" out of too much. Don't give in to "the vultures" any longer. You will find the effort worth it. "The worm has turned." You are in for "a whale of" a life and soon be able to "wolf down" the pleasures of the good times.

Perhaps, the list below is a more sensible approach to considering animal expressions.

Expressions

Albatross, around your neck
Alligator, see you later
Ants, in your pants
Ape, hairy as an
Ass, don't let anyone make an, of you, the law is an
Badger, don't, me
Badger game, a form of blackmail
Bat, blind as a bat
Bear, loaded for, hungry as a
Bears, of Wall Street
Beastly, unpleasant
Beaver, busy as a beaver, a tall hat
Bee, make a line, in your bonnet, busy as a
Bird, early bird catches the worm, eats like, love, of a feather flock together
Birdies, in badminton
Buck the trend, young
Bug eyed, cute as, snug as in a rug
Buffalo, to be buffaloed, intimidated
Bull, in a china shop, your way, market, sling the, eye, grab by the horns,
Bunnies, dumb
Butterflies, social, in your stomach
Buzzard, old
Camel, the straw that broke the, back
Canary, cat that swallowed the
Cat, cool, nap, seat, pajamas, cradle, catbird seat
Chicken, spring, feed, with their heads cut off, out
Cam up, happy as a
Cock, sure, eyed

Coot, old, crazy as
Cow, how now brown cow, holy
Crab, finding fault,
Crane, Machine for lifting heavy weight
Cricket, an English game, fair play
Crocodile, tears
Crow, eat, as the flies, old, to brag
Cuckoo, an idiom fool, crazy
Deer, run like a deer
Dipper, a vessel for transferring liquid
Dog, days, fight, leg, eared, tag, trot, doggy paddle, in the doghouse
Dog meat, worthless
Donkey, donkey's years
Duck, dead as a, like water off of
Eagle, eye, two under par
Eel, slippery as an
Elephant (ine), portions, memory of
Feathers, ruffle your
Fish, cold, for compliments, drink like, or cut bait in troubled waters
Flies, catch more flies with honey than with Vinegar
Flounder, around
Fox, out, sly as
Frog, leap, in your throat
Gander, take a
Goat, scape, get his, one taking blame for another
Goose, loose as a, silly as a, don't kill the golden egg, cooked, feed gasoline to an engine
Goose step, a high step
Gopher, to plow, to go after
Grasshopper, knee-high to a, what's sauce for is sauce for the gander,
Gull- ible, naive, easy to trick
Guinea pig, experimenter
Hare, brained
Hawk, your wares, to pursue, peddler
Hen, mad as a wet hen
Hen pecked, under influence of a spouse
Herring, red a diversion from the main issue

Hog, high on the, eat like a, wild as, go whole, the limelight, gluttonous, greedy selfish
Hornet, stir up a hornets nest
Horse, around, of a different color, feathers, meat, fly, you can lead to water - you can't make him drink, to put on airs, sense
Horsepower, look a gift in the mouth, work like a, beat a dead
Hounds, hunt with the hounds
Jackass, stupid, ignorant
Kite, flown at the end of a string
Kitten, nervous as a
Kitty litter, pot in poker
Lamb, gentle as a
Lamb baste, give a thrashing
Lark, happy as a
Lion, get the lions share beard the
Lobster, red as, an awkward person
Mackerel, holy, exclamation
Mole hill, make a mountain of, a protrusion on the human body
Monkey, wrench, money, stock, a vessel, container
Monkey around playful
Mouse, quiet as, a bruise under the eye
Mule, stubborn as
Owl, wise as an
Ox, whose is being gored, strong as
Oyster, the world is my
Parrot, talk-repeat or intimidate without understanding, to be vain, to strut
Partridge, plump as
Peacock, strutting
Penguin suit, a dinner jacket
Pig, headed, out, eats like a, fat as a, live in a pigsty, football, in a poke
Pigeon, stool, hole, a simpleton, dud, easy to deceive
Pony, a glass, girl's pigtail
Possum, play, pretend, feign illness or death
Puppy, hush
Rabbit, multiply like, a dish of melted cheese and toast
Rail, fence, railroad, a robe or dress
Ram, a plunger, to stuff or cram, to strike with great force.

Rat, race
Rat, on, sneaky contemptible person, pack
Scallop, serrated, a series of cuts on cloth
Sardines, packed like
Seal, to fasten secure, tightly
Shark, swindler, cheat sharply, expert
Sheep, black, silly, stupid, meek, timid, diploma
Shrew, a scolding nagging evil-tongued woman
Shrimp, small insignificant person
Skunk, to defeat overwhelmingly/preventing score
Skunk, drunk as a, inebriated
Sloth, delay, slowness, laziness, idleness
Slug, to take a drink, to hit, a coin
Snake, in the grass
Snails, pace, lazy slow moving person
Sow, you can't make a silk purse out of a, ear
Squirrel, away, hide, hoard,
Swallow, to take in, absorb, to refrain from expressing
Swan, song, ending
Swift, fast, fleet, ready, hasty, quick, speedy
Tiger, a smart boy-groom, a cruel person
Tiger paper, a sham show of power
Toad, a person who is the object of contempt
Turkey, tough, talk, neck, cold, failure, to talk candidly, blunt
Vulture, any greedy or ruthless person
Weasel, out of, words cunning, sly
Whale, of an appetite, having great capacity; to thrash, beat/lash
Wolf, a male who flirts aggressively with woman
Wolf, down, consume a lot in short order lone,
Wolf, keep from the door, avoid hardship
Worm, turns, times change
Woodcock, a simpleton, a fool

You can get an argument of where and how formal languages got their start. We know for sure at one time communication was only by pictorial design, gestures, and a few grunts. Ancient man communicated with signals, sign language, symbols and drawings. Until man developed language systems the world of discourse was one of charades.

Words were developed by necessity. Today over 3,000 languages exist around the globe. At the same time there is evidence we are returning full cycle to the early methods of interplay. Some estimates of communication without words or using abbreviations are as high as 70%. The change is apparent in all areas of our daily real life. Short form communication is once again on the rise especially with the younger generation.

Animals have played a lead role in both modes. The English language is swarming with animal words. It seems that almost every common animal in our midst has attached its name to some verb or noun. One can be dogged in the pursuit of something, and pig out when you get it. You can snake through to get somewhere, and horse around when you get there.

Notwithstanding so many words originating from the animal kingdom they get their message across with each other through onomatopoeia. Listen to the call of the bird, the bark of the dog, the meow of the cat, and the moo of the cow. Whether vocal, mechanical, mobile or static-terrestrial, animals have an effective ways of signaling danger, displaying mating rituals, establishing territory, and showing love and affection to humans; obviously all accomplished without words.

Visit a zoo and see their show-off and stand-off antics. The gorilla thumping his chest, monkeys scurrying about in the acrobatic act, prairie dogs doing their comedy routine, a lion roaring his dominate. Hear the growl of the grizzly or pick up the scent of a skunk, hear a rooster crowing, the bugle of the moose, watch the display of the peacock's tail or the vibrations of a rattlesnake. It's another of their ways of communicating without words.

Observing the effective means of exchange without words certainly contributes to our move toward sign language. Another factor is that so many words have more than one meaning. The word "set" for example has over 100 definitions and "run" is a close second.

Animals haven't escaped this phenomenon as indicated below. Few conversations are held without the name of an animal entering the discourse. The message sent may be totally foreign to anything pertaining directly to the named creature. Some are well-known and others obscure either by implication or from little use.

Alligator, one who is singing
Ape, bush, a worker in the country
Ass, dull, stupid
Badger to tease, overdraw one's account
Badger, game, a form of blackmail
Bat, speed, hit, a stick or racket
Bear, carry weight, growl like, stocks
Beastly, unpleasant
Beaver, tall hat, one who pitches in eagerly
Bee in the bonnet, have an obsession, queer ideas
Beetle a jutting, overhanging
Bird, clay pigeon, shuttlecock, of a feather
Bird cage, a woman's dress, small box, a wire
Birdie golf term for one under par
Bitch to complain
Bittern, liquid remaining from salt crystallization
Buffalo, bamboozle, to intimidate, to confuse
Bug, whiskey, small compact automobile
Bull, false story, small keg
Butterfly, a swimmers breast stroke
Calf, a meek harmless brainless person
Camel, a cylinder used for raising sunken ships
Canary, written promise of a donation
Cardinal, mulled red wine, high priest
Carp brag
Cat, a tripod having 6 feet, a machine, market, many persons talking at the same time, nap, out of the bag, to disclose a secret or trick, walk a brick paved pathway, long plank
Cat gut, sheep intestines dried for string
Cattle, black gathering of clergy
Chicken, feeble, scared, coward, feed; small change, a pittance
Clam, upon who says very little
Colt, newcomer
Cormorant, greedy person glutton
Cow, a wedged shaped brake (mining)
Cow and calf, to laugh
Cow cow, to be in rage, to scold

Cow hitch, a poorly tied knot
Cow juice, milk
Crab, complain, sideward drift (nautical)
Crane, machine for lifting heavy weights
Cricket, an English game, fair play
Crow, brag
Cuckoo, an idiot, fool, crazy
Dipper, a vessel for transferring water
Dog, black, counterfeit silver coin, put on the, to be false
Dog fight, until one is overcome
Dog cheap, exceedingly cheap
Dog leg, curved
Dog meat, worthless
Dog tag, identification disc
Dolphin, a spar or buoy
Donkey, ride the to cheat with weights and measures, years
Duck move to avoid
Ducks on the pond (men on base (baseball)
Eagle two under par (golf)
Eagle eye, having good vision, a locomotive engineer
Ferret, pawnbroker, barge thief, to cheat
Fish, to grope for, find and bring into view, to fry
Fish eyes, tapioca pudding
Fish hooks, fingers
Fish horn, a soprano clarinet
Fox, slyly, watch closely, to sham, trick, deceive
Fox drunk, crafty drunk
Fox trot, dance
Frog, policeman on foot, scabbard loop
Giraffe, an 18th century spinet, mining incline car
Goat, one taking the blame for others. lecher, not conventional, a fool
Goatee, tufted beard
Goats wool, something nonexistent
Goldfinch, rich man
Goose, to hiss at, feed gasoline to an engine, hangs high everything is lovely-all is well, honk like a, plod, tailors soothing iron, a high step
Gopher, a plow, a waffle

Grasshopper an airplane used for scouting & observation
Greyhound, a speedy ocean steamer
Grouse, complain, grumble
Guinea-pig, experimenter
Gull, to gulp, swallow
Hare, to run fast, harass, scare
Hawk, to pursue, spit with difficulty and noise
Hawker, peddler
Hawks, an advantage
Hen, cackle like a
Hen pecked, husband under wife's influence
Hog road, wild, greedy, gluttonous, selfish
Horse, to possess a woman
Horse, ride the high, to put on airs
Horse talk, talk big, boastingly
Horse away to spend in a lottery
Horse sense, common sense
Jackass, stupid, ignorant
Jellyfish, spineless
Kite flown at the end of a string, greedy grasping person, highest sails of ship
Kitten, a pint or 1/2 pint pewter pot
Kitty, pot in poker
Lamb baste, give a thrashing
Lion's den, headmasters study
Lobster, cry, an awkward person
Mole, a spot protuberance on the human body
Monkey, money, stock; a vessel, container
hammer for ship building, soldering liquid
Monkey brand often applied to an ugly face
Monkey grease useless
Monkey shines monkey like antics or tricks
Mouse knot made on a rope, bruise under the eye
Otter, a sailor
Ounce, unit of measurement
Owl, a blow or punch, night train
Parrot, to repeat or imitate without understanding
Peacock, to be vain; to strut

Pelican, a hatchet; an instrument for pulling teeth
Penguin suit, a dinner jacket
Pheasant, silver, a beautiful woman of society
Pica, a category of type
Pig, greedy; filthy; casting of iron, six pence, policeman, a garment
Pig by the ear, a mistake
Pig in a poke a blind bargain
Pig skin, saddle, football
Pig sty, the press room, an abode
Pigeon, simpleton, a dud; easy to deceive
Pigeon hole, gap between two words, a study
Pony, a glass, girl's pigtail, pay up
Possum play pretend, feign illness or death
Quail pipe, a woman's tongue
Rabbit, a dish of melted cheese and toast, inferior player of any game buy the, to have the worse of a bargain
Rabbit foot, good luck
Rail, fence; by railroad, a robe or dress
Ram plunger; the striking part of a pile, driver, to stuff or cram; to strike with great force
Rat to steal or rob, sneaky contemptible person, stool pigeon
Rat it run away quickly
Rat, pack, collector
Rat tail, a legal writ
Rats in the loft eccentric, mad
Reptile, sneaky, mean; creepy, crawling
Rhea, fifth satellite of Saturn
Scallop, serrated, a series of curves on cloth
Seal, something that closes fastens tightly
Shark, adept, expert, a swindler, cheat, to get by fraud
Sheep, silly, stupid, meek, timid, defenseless
Sheep gut, sold, a term of contempt
Sheep walk, a prison
Sheep skin, diploma
Shrew, a scolding nagging evil-tongued woman, evil, a malign, danger
Shrimp, a small insignificant person
Skunk, to defeat overwhelmingly/preventing score, a despicable person

Sloth, delay, slowness, laziness, idleness
Slug, to be slow or lazy; to hit; a single drink, a piece of metal as a coin
Snail, lazy slow moving person, one of the striking, work of a clock
Snake, a skein of silk, to steal something, to pull quickly, pull jerk or haul
Snake, give, to vex, annoy
Snake juice, whiskey
Spider, a trivet, frying pan, cultivating tool
Squirrel to store, hide, hoard; carding machine roller
Swallow, to take in, absorb, refrain from expressing, to put up with, to accept
Swift, fast, fleet, ready, hasty, quick, speedy
Tiger, a smart boy-groom, a cruel person
Toad, a person who is the object of contempt
Tortoise, a testudo (moveable shelter)
Turkey, failure, to talk candidly, bluntly
Vampire, a person who preys ruthlessly on others
Vulture, any greedy or ruthless person
Weasel, cunning, sly
Whale, having great capacity; to thrash, beat/lash
Wheatear, an ear of wheat
Wolf, a male who flirts aggressively to devour ravenously
Woodcock, a simpleton, a fool

The many words and expressions that originated in one form or another from animals are not always apparent. Some are more direct than others. When the animal's name is given it's easy but several expressions are disguised. A cross section of this veiled group that is easily overlooked is reviewed below.

Adding Insult to Injury

In Aesop's fable "The Bald Man and the Fly" a fly bites the head of a bald man who then, trying to crush the insect with his hand, misses the fly and smacks himself on the head. The fly says, "You wanted to avenge the sting of a tiny insect with death what will you do to yourself, now that you have *added insult to injury*?

Adulate

In ancient Rome, the Latin word *adularia* meant "to fawn upon like a dog", hence "to flatter servility." The word went from Latin into French forms and then into English. Today, to flatter or admire excessively is *to adulate*.

Arctic

The frigid north region gets its name from a familiar northern constellation-the polar bear, in a fashion. Arctic goes back to Greek *arktos*, meaning "bear." The ancient Greeks included the stars we know as the Big Dipper as part of a larger constellation that they called the *Arktos Megale*, literally "Great Bear." The Greek name was translated into Latin as *Ursa Major*, which is still the term that modern astronomers use for the constellation today.

Auspicious

With the advent of Christianity, the only instance of divination from birds came in the story of the dove at Jesus' baptism. The word auspicious is one of the words that came out of this bird study by the ancients. If the birds were flying in the right way, then the day was considered auspicious: a good one in which to start some project. The word literally means "bird watcher."

We all know that some of our politicians are "for the birds" and even bird-brained, but science has shown that birds fly lower to the ground before a storm.

What birds are eating can also give you an idea of the conditions of the land.

Bangs

The term we now use to describe a particular hairstyle comes from the way a horse's tail looked! Money problems in the middle of the nineteenth century hurt the rich sportsmen. Some sold their stables and horses. Others merely reduced their staff and kept only their best animals. The shorthanded stable crews couldn't groom horses as carefully as before. It had been customary to spend hours trimming a horse's tail: in the new age of austerity, grooms just cut the tail off square, or "banged it off".

Soon bangtail animals were winning horse races everywhere. Designers took note, and it wasn't long before women were displaying their hair in bangs.

Barnacle

The word comes from a devise for restraining a horse that pinched its nose between two branches joined by a hinge. Also for an instrument of human torture applied in a similar way. Later, spectacles (because they pinch the nose) acquired the name barnacles. This is a completely different barnacle from the one we know that accumulates on ships and other matter.

Bat one's eye

When we wink especially in surprise or emotion we are said *to bat*. In this sense, it comes form the *bate* referring to hawks and meaning to flap the wings wildly.

Beat around the bush

A popular English sport was called batfowling-hunting birds at night. Batfowlers beat the bushes with a stick to rouse them to flight into a net.

Bite

When a fish seizes or snaps at the bait of a angler, it is said to bite. Fugitively, among humans, to respond so as to be caught by a trick of any kind is to *bite*.

Blubber

Blubber is the fat of whales and other large marine mammals. Excessive fat on humans has also come to be called *blubber*.

Bone of Contention

A bone often causes a fight between dogs. Today, anything that creates a conflict or an argument is more specifically call a *bone of contention.*

Bone to pick

A dog often spends a great deal of time and effort chewing on a bone. Therefore, anything that occupies a person was once called a *bone to pick.* The phrase has also meant a difficulty to solve. Today a grievance or appoint of contention *is a bone to pick.*

Bridle

When the reins on a horse are abruptly pulled, the animal will react with a sharp upward movement of its head. The reins are part of the bridle. Therefore, among humans, to tuck in the chin and throw back the head as in protest or vanity or scorn is *to bridle.* Or broadly, to give any evidence of hostility is *to bridle.*

To browse:

Grass-hungry animals of medieval Europe often resorted to nibbling on leaves and twigs of shrubs, even low trees. From an old term for "young shoot," the deer or ox that ate such stuff was said to *browse.*

Farmers who took their stock with them into the American frontier were sometimes hard pressed in winter. After hay was exhausted, cattle were turned out to browse. The nature of the coarse provender was such that a browsing animal seldom ate steadily at one spot. Instead there was sporadic nibbling and much moving about from place to place in search of something better.

It was probably an author, huffy over treatment of his books, who first compared halfhearted readers with cows moving from shrub to shrub. Once the vivid resemblance was seen, however, it quickly became proverbial. As a result, many a library that owns neither a cow nor a goat is equipped with a special room for use by patrons who like to browse.

Bury one's head in the sand

This expression is based on the false belief that an ostrich will bury its head in the sand to avoid danger. The bird's habit of lowering its long neck to avoid detection while hatching or protecting its young is responsible for our use today to explain one that is trying to avoid reality or to ignore facts.

Come to the end of one's rope:

An animal tied to a stake can graze only as far as the rope will go. Sometimes an animal trying to reach beyond the end of the rope will stretch and strain and practically choke itself to death. But, of course, the animal usually fails and gets nothing for the effort but frustration and exhaustion. Figuratively, among humans, to reach the limit of one's energy or ability is *to come to (or be at) the end of one's rope.*

Coward:

The tail is a very timid member of an animal. When frightened they may draw their tail between their hind legs, or simply turn its tail and run. In such an animal as the hare, the white flash of the fleeing tail is especially remarkable. But even a tailless animal like man can turn tail and flee when afraid. And it is in the tail of an army, unless that army is in retreat that you can expect to find the cowards.

Whether it is the idea of an animal's tail or an army's retreat that is responsible, it is certain that the Old French cuart or coart, from which we get our coward, is a derivative of coe or coue, tail.

Cranberry

Cranberries acquired their name from the Low German *Krangeere*, meaning "crane," because the plant flourishes in marshy lands frequented by cranes.

Earmark:

Originally from ear + mark a cut or mark in the ear of sheep and cattle, serving as a sign of ownership (stamp of ownership).

Eat humble pie

This is one of those expressions that came about from confusion. Umbles are the internal organs (heart, liver, and so on) of an animal; especially a deer. A variant spelling of umbles is humbles. People used to make a dish called humble pie, a pie made of umbles. The pie was thought to be an inferior food. To eat humble pie was to demonstrate one's modest circumstances. Because of that literal sense of humble pie and because of a confusion with, or a consciously humorous reference to, the unrelated word humble meaning meek or lowly, people said that to be submissive or apologetic of humiliate is to eat *humble pie.*

Get one's back up

An angry cat will arch its back. Therefore, to become angry is to *get one's back up.*

Go belly up

When a fish dies, it will often float with its belly up. Figuratively, to experience any failure is to *go belly up.*

Groom

To attend to the cleaning of an animal, is to groom it. Extended to humans, or to things, to groom means to give them a neat appearance. Further extended, to groom people means to prepare them for something (such as politics); and to refine something (such as language) is to *groom* it.

Halter

A halter is a device of rope or leather straps by which an animal can be led or secured. Transferred to humans, halter means a rope with a noose for execution by hanging. Halter also means execution itself. To hamper or restrain is to halter plus the one you first thought of.

Hands down

In the ninth century horseracing, the phrase to "win hands down" referred to the jockey dropping his hands and relaxing his hold on the reins when victory appeared certain. Today, to do anything easily or without question is to do it *hands down.*

Hobson's choice

Tobias (or Thomas) Hobson was an English liveryman who lived in the late 1500s and early 1600s. He was known for forcing his customers to take the horse nearest the door or none at all. Therefore, an apparently free choice when there is no real alternative is a *Hobson's' choice.*

Hue and cry

On the surface, the phrase hue and cry does not betray its use in early law-enforcement methods. But it came into being because medieval yeomen considered it great sport to hunt down criminals as though they were wild beasts.

Hunters of the period took their sport seriously and developed special cries to be used in pursuing various kinds of game. Consequently, by listening to the clamor of the chase, persons at a distance could tell whether the quarry was a deer, fox, boar, or other animal.

The legal system of the age gave accused persons few rights, so thy frequently tried to escape rather than face trial. In such instances the sheriff and his men brought hounds and literally staged a manhunt. As they rode through the forest on the trails the fugitive, they would give a distinctive hue and cry in order to arouse the whole countryside. Upon hearing it, every honest citizen was supposed to drop his work and join in the chase.

Inaugurate

We commonly associate this word with the swearing in celebration of a new office holder. In ancient Rome the word meant something entirely different.

Among the many things an augur would do before recommending whether or not you should do something is to check the way the birds were flying. These almost magical soothsayers would tell a general not to march on one day or do battle on another by the formations of the birds on the wing. They might even catch one and cut it open to observe its entrails or omens. "Inauguration" was completed before determining whether or not to begin any major venture.

Kite

The kite was once Britain's most common bird of prey. Almost any day a person could look up and see one of these graceful birds gliding with the wind. The kite would spread its wings and drift overhead looking for a rodent to prey on.

About the beginning of the seventeenth century, English children learned to make a wooden frame which they stretched paper tightly across. When they pulled it with a sting, it gained altitude and fluttered about much like the kite. So it was natural that it should be called a kite.

Litter

The word litter goes back to Latin *lectus*, ("bed"). Animal bedding (litter) was often straw, paper or other loose material that covered the floor. The term came to mean to scatter (things) in disorder, without reference to a bed.

Lock horns

Various types of deer were familiar to early European hunters and sportsmen. They were a favorite quarry of kings and noblemen during England's age of chivalry.

Still, adventurers of later eras who left the island kingdom for New England were quite unprepared to see their first moose. Standing seven feet high at the withers, an old bull may boast antlers weighing as much as sixty pounds.

Though males are shy and unapproachable during most of the year, they become aggressive during the autumn mating season. Two big fellows sometimes stage a battle over a drab little cow, fighting savagely with horns and hooves. Nature offers few spectacles as grim as that of such giant swains with their spreading horns locked in battle.

Frontier speech was quickly enriched by comparing angry opponents with battling moose No matter how smooth their heads, persons who clash violently are said to *lock horns*.

Land on one's foot

No matter how a cat fails, it always seems to land safely on its feet. That observation has long been applied figuratively to humans, so that to remain safe or successful after going through a hardship is to land on one's feet (or legs).

Mad as a hatter

Until just before the Industrial Revolution, masculine headgear was made almost exclusively of animal skins.

In order to increase the felting properties of hides used in making hats, mercury was extensively employed in the tanning process. Hat makers handling furs many hours a day over a period of years, gradually absorbed the poisonous metal. Consequently, many hatters began to suffer from the shakes in early middle age. A few years later mental disturbances would begin.

So it became proverbial to speak of any peculiar or unbalanced person as *mad as a hatter*. Popularized by Lewis Carroll, the expression entered the language-apparently to stay.

Off one's feed

When an animal loses its appetite, as from illness, it is said to be off its feed. For humans it is the same and additionally the expression has also been extended to include emotional as well as physical troubles, so that to be depressed is to be *off one's feed.*

Off the hook

If a hooked fish manages to escape, it has obviously been freed from a perilous situation. That has been extended to humans when they rid a difficult situation or responsibility they are *off the hook*.

Peck

In its original reference to birds, to peck means to strike, or to pick up food, with the beak. That has passed to humans to explain to strike with repeated small movements-on the good side think kiss. The expression also is used to mean to eat sparingly or to criticize constantly.

Pester:

Although a person who pesters is called a pest the two words are etymologically unrelated, but still animal related. Pest is a derivative of Latin pestis, 'plaque', and pester of Latin pastor, 'herdsman', shepherd'. The Middle French word empestrer meant 'to hobble (an animal). It is derived, via a hypothetical popular Medieval Latin verb impastoriare, from pastoria, a term found in ignited, a tether for a grazing horse (to shackle the feet at pasture).

Pastoria in turn comes from the Latin adjective pastorius, of 'a a herdsman', which would take the form pastoria when identifying a feminine noun such as chorda 'cord' or catena chain'.

The Middly French word empestrer developed, from the original meaning 'to hobble', the extended sense 'to impede'. This was the meaning of the sixteenth-century English borrowing pester. Under the influence of the remarkably but accidentally similar noun pest, pester acquired the further sense' to annoy'.

The plaque connotation giving a higher degree of annoyance is probably better represented in the continuance of that origin with our present day pestilence any virulent or fatal contagious disease; an epidemic.

Pie

Until the late eighteenth century, the bird now called magpie was termed simply "pie". Then as now, such a bird was likely to be a habitual collector. It was not unusual to find a pie's nest filled with pebbles, bits of broken glass, string, chicken feathers, and so on.

At some unrecorded time, an inspired housewife thought of placing a crust around a small pot of stew. She used whatever ingredients were at hand-meat, fowl, or fish, plus a few vegetables and perhaps an egg or two. Her men folk liked the odd conglomeration and, casting about for a name, compared it with a pie's nest, which was filled with a variety of odds and ends. So they called the new dish *pie.*

First used in writing around 1303, the word came to include many varieties of pie. No other language has a word that is even distantly related to the name of the most popular of English dishes.

Pitted against

To set animals into a pit to fight each other is to pit them. From that practice the idea of saying that, among humans, to be set in opposition is to be *pitted against.*

Puce

The color, puce (deep red to a dark gray grayish purple), comes from the French word for "flea." Puce and the English word flea are distant cousins, for they both ultimately descend from the same Indo-European root. *Puce* comes from Old French *pulce,* which descends form Latin *pulex. Pulex,* in turn is a descendant of the Indo-European root plou-, meaning "flea."

Puss

Originally, from Dutch and Low German and imitative of the spitting noise of a cat, became a call-name for cats in the 16th century and during the next hundred years, a slang word for girl or woman. The derivation of *puss* as slang for "face" is from the Gaelic pus and earlier buss, for "lip" whence also sourpuss, for a scowling expression, and by extension for a grouchy disposition.

Put out to pasture

It is common to place an animal, such as a workhorse, in old age or in poor health away from their work and literally put the out to pasture. It is natural to refer to a human in retirement as being *put out to pasture.*

Root

When animals, particularly swine, turn up or dig in the earth for food it is said they root. The term transfers to humans when they poke about to discover or search. The pig part doesn't make the same transit.

Rule the Roost

A roost is a bird's nesting place Extended beyond relation *roost* means any place for sitting, resting or staying. To be in charge of a place (as a rooster controls the chicken roost) is to *rule the roost.* This is an Americanized version of the much older British expression *to rule the roost,* of obscure origin. Some advise to be careful who rules the rooster.

Ruminate

The word ruminate has a dual animal connection. Mostly used in the meaning "to consider" it also has a technical background in animal husbandry, "to chew the cud."

Ruminate comes from Latin *ruminare,* which meant both "to chew the cud" (when used of animals) and "to medicate" (when used of people), just as its English descendant. The Latin verb in turn is derived from the noun *rumen,* "gullet, a word that was applied in particular to the large first stomach of ruminant animals that have four stomachs." It may be difficult to digest the double meaning but take comfort in the fact that the chew the cud reference is rarely used today.

Slow and steady wins the race

This expression is a way of saying that careful, constant effort will accomplish more than hurried, sporadic effort. It comes from Aesop's fable "The Hare and the Tortoise."

Sour grapes

Another of Aesop's fables figured into this expression. The fox who couldn't reach a bunch of grapes consoled himself by saying that the fruit was probably sour anyhow. Disparagement of getting something desired but unattainable is now called *sour grapes*.

Spur

From Old English *spura, spora,* "spur is a metal implement worn on the heel to goad a horse. The term is related to *spurnam*a "to kick," and has support from several languages including Proto-Germanic *spuron*, Old Norse *spori*, Middle Dutch *spore*, Dutch spoor, Old High German *Sporn*, and German *spornm*,

Stampede

Stampede comes from Mexican Spanish *estampida*, a word that originally meant "explosion, bang, crash, uproar." American Spanish changed that to mean a sudden rush of animals, such as cattle and horses. In the mid -1800s the term came to be used for miners rushing westward to find gold in the California gold rush.

Tacky

An inferior horse is often called a tacky. Today we take that start to describe something shabby or lacking in good taste.

Trap

A devise for catching game or other animals applies to humans when they are caught or stopped (literally or figuratively) unaware.

Vaccine

The word vaccine has an unusual animal connection. It comes from Latin *vacca*, "cow," a descendant of French *vache* and Spanish *vaca*.

Before the days of vaccinations, the dread disease smallpox caused a lot of deaths. Survivors often had terrible disfiguring scars. Dr. Edward Jenner observed that people who had caught cowpox, a mild disease caught from dairy cows, did not get smallpox afterward. The doctor took liquid from the smallpox sores of a milkmaid and injected a boy with it. Two weeks later, he exposed the boy to smallpox and luckily the boy remained healthy.

The same type experiment might not be possible today but it was effective.

Under one's skin

Mites, ticks and some other insects embed themselves under the skin of their victims and cause itching and irritation. It naturally when one is irritated or deeply affected by someone or something to explain their situation the same- *under one's skin.*

Under the wire

The origin of this expression has its root in horse-racing. American racetracks in the latter part of the nineteenth century—before the days of cameras—had a wire strung across the track above the finishing line to help stewards decide which nose had got across the line first.

An early example appeared in Scribner's Magazine in July 1889. "As the end of the stand was reached Timarch worked up to Petrel, and the two raced down to the 'wire,' cheered on by the applause of the spectators. They ended the first half mile of the race head and head, passing lapped together under the wire, and beginning in earnest the mile which was yet to be traversed". So, a race that was undecided until the very last moment was said to go down to the wire.

Well-heeled:

To arm a gamecock with a gaff, an artificial spur of metal, used as a weapon, is *to heel* the bird. Hence, in American slang of the late 1800s, to furnish with anything, in particular to supply with a gun, was to heel. Today, the reference is specifically to money, so that to be well supplied with money is to be *well-heeled.*

Another obstacle to communication comes from the fact we have so many words that look alike and so many other words that are spelled the same, but have different meanings. It's no wonder we get confused. Comprehension of the English language doesn't become any less complicated with animal involvement.

The sentences that follow demonstrate this impediment with a distinctive insight from an animal's standpoint. It may be comforting to know that they too experience predicament with our vernacular.

The adder is reported to be a calculating snake.
How silly to walk around with an albatross around your neck.
His awkwardness reminded me of an auk trying to climb a Yew tree.
It is unwise to badger a badger
Don't drive like a bat out of hell, especially if you are blind as a bat.
Bears can be unbearable and your will have to bear the brunt of their attack.
A bed bug can disturb your sleep.
If you feel a bee in your bonnet it is best to make a beeline for water.
A boar is no bore.
A spoiled feline sleeps on satin sheets and has its own cat-a-pillow.
A catacomb doesn't have anything to do with feline grooming.
Anyway you get buffaloed it hurts.
Hitting a bull's eye can be dangerous.
I read where the cardinal rule for the cardinal is for it to be red.
The chicken is chicken to take on the wolf.
It doesn't pay for a cow to beef.
The cow did not utter a sound when the calf approached the udder.
It is better to crab at another than to claw them.
Barking up the wrong tree does not have to involve a dog.
The boxer is a prize winning dog, who may never enter a ring.
You are likely to get dogged if you hound too much.
When you feel dog-tired at night, it may be because you growled and grumbled all day.
A duck bill doesn't have to be paid.
A lame duck may have to swim uphill.
An elk will wolf down a coyote after the kill.
A finch will flinch if you pinch its nose.
A suckerfish will succor its young to obtain sucker.
Many who flounder continue to fish for compliments.
A flower frog can't jump.

The croak of the frog is much less drastic than that of man.

The gnu knew better than to mess with the new member of the herd.

A goat can also have 2-legs.

A tin can can make a goat gloat.

A goose egg can be nothing.

Fighting a gorilla would be a thrilla.

The gull has the gull to gulp the fisherman's catch.

Its pouch does not hamper a hamster.

Big ears allow the hare to hear.

Hawk your day as a hawk would its prey.

When trimming a hedgehog use long shears.

Horse sense is stable thinking; it's what keeps horses from betting on what people will do.

You can't win the race of life by horsing around.

The horse brayed when the braid of roses was placed over his head.

A jackal may have been the first to build a jackal.

Lion down on the job doesn't pay.

To be the spitting image of a llama is not the highest compliment.

A lynx was spotted on the links, he had broken through the links of the old chain fence.

Magpie is for the birds.

The titi monkey doesn't hide in the titi tree.

Monkey business is usually not profitable.

A moose has a morose expression.

It's unlikely nether the moose or mouse eats mousse for desert.

An ox bow is not a knot or an animal.

An oyster spat is not disagreeable.

A bouquet of pheasants doesn't have anything to do with flowers.

Eating pheasant is pleasant except if you're a pheasant.

Be careful in which pigeon hole you store your papers.

Pigs are hamstrung.

In a pig's eye, buying a pig in a poke is not a good idea.

The pipefish is neither a musician nor a smoker.

A porcupine doesn't come from a pig tree.

Silver fish have relatives on land by the same name.

Some farmers are prone to rail when a rail sits on their rail.

A rail makes better time by flight than a train by rail.

A ram really knows how to ram home its point.
The ray fish swims better at night with a ray of light shining.
Some claim that fish roe is the favorite food of the roe.
You would never see a sable wearing a sable at a funeral.
The sea lion can see under water.
A seal seals out water with oily skin.
Shellfish are said to be selfish seafood.
One shrew deserves another.
Not all shrimps are shrimps.
Skunks must be smart; they have a lot of scents.
The skunk is a very instinctive animal.
You can't act like a skunk without someone getting wind of it.
Smelt smell fishy.
The ore smelt smelled worse than a dead smelt.
A spot can spot a meal from a distance.
The squirrel is nuts about squirreling away his food.
A stag affair does not have to include animals.
The swift flew above the swift current.
A tapir is a tapered rhinoceros.
The tapir has a taper to its nose.
You won't see a thrush with thrush.
A tick in the tick can keep you awake.
I saw a toad being towed into the water by a frog.
A tumbler doesn't drink from a tumbler.
A weasel will never try to weasel out of its responsibility.
It is said that whales wail when in Wales.
A wildcat strike hurts either way.
We have 100% proof the wolver/wine can be intoxicating.

In this next part, find a game designed to open your eyes and ears to the joys of homophony.

Fun and games with homonyms.

Each of the following clues should lead you to a phrase consisting of two homophones. All are related to the animal kingdom.

Example: A naked grizzly is a bare bear. Give them a try before going to the answers.

1. female deer sleep ____________ ____________
2. raspy throated equine ____________ ____________
3. insect relative ____________ ____________
4. tiresome pig ____________ ____________
5. cry from the largest mammal ____________ ____________
6. rabbit fur ____________ ____________
7. stinking chicken ____________ ____________
8. fighting ape ____________ ____________
9. precious buck ____________ ____________
10. antlered animal's desert ____________ ____________
11. dragged cousin of the frog ____________ ____________
12. inexpensive chick's cry ____________ ____________
13. wildcat's chain parts ____________ ____________
14. smoked salmon fastenings ____________ ____________
15. mollusk brawn ____________ ____________
16. horrible bear ____________ ____________
17. runs from insects ____________ ____________
18. donkey whimper ____________ ____________
19. recently acquired antelope ____________ ____________
20. female sheep utilize ____________ ____________
21. animal feet stop ____________ ____________
22. line of fish eggs ____________ ____________
23. flock listened ____________ ____________
24. appendage story ____________ ____________
25. small insect power ____________ ____________
26. buy bird stations ____________ ____________
27. encounter animal flesh ____________ ____________

The text below pauses to reflect on how animal's versatility affects our thinking. The first has items giving food for thought; statements giving a distinctive insight from an animals' standpoint.

Next, a number of statements to ponder; another way of showing animals also experience predicament with our vernacular. Allow your mind to wander about animal's significance as you contemplate the queries made.

The honey is sweet but the bee has a sting.

The bee is praised, the mosquito swatted.

Birds have bills, but they keep on singing.

Robert Feline is more commonly known as a bobcat.

I'm over the hump, said the camel.

Be like a dog biting its tail. Make both ends meet.

Ducks send a good message. Keep calm and unruffled on the surface, but paddle like crazy underneath.

Don't tell fish stories where people know you, but particularly don't tell them where they know the fish.

The blowfish has a swell personality.

Frogs have it easy. They can eat what bugs them.

Giraffes have the right idea. Stick your neck out and reach higher than all the others.

Be like a horse with some horse sense-stable thinking and the ability to san "nay."

Don't horse around, sowing your wild oats can be dangerous.

An individual who is a leech can usually worm out of anything.

Avoid being like the lemming. Don't follow the crowd and jumping to conclusions.

Follow the lion. Live life with pride and grab the lion's share with might and main.

A llama is a camel whose hump has been bumped.

Church mice may be poor, but they are religious.

Evolution is the assent of man from monkey, which some people forget to make.

The lesson of the owl is worthwhile. Be wise but still give a hoot.

It's not true that owls don't give a hoot.

A rabbit's foot is a poor substitute for horse sense.

Sardines live a cramped life.

Snakes beware when the mongoose is on the loose.

Storks run a mom and pop delivery service.

The termite is a boring animal.

Some trumpeters play in the water, some in the air, and others with air.

Turtles are mild mannered and self-contained.

It's no wonder turtlenecks are warm.

If you talk turkey, you may end up being gobbled up in the conversation.

Whale's personality is reported to have a blow hard tenancy.
Beware of the wolf wearing wool.
Emulate the woodpecker. Just keep pecking away until you finish the job. You'll succeed by using your head

We are confronted with Questions as soon as we learn to speak. Spend a day with a 2-year old and see how the concept works. Since most animals have not learned to speak liberty is taken to make inquiry in their behalf. Allow your mind to wander about animal's habits, characteristics, and mannerisms and how they contributed to man's development. Some, certainly not all, will provide a better insight to the process. It might be well that animals are unable to communicate their answers.

Can ants in your pants be let out through the fly?
Do bees groom their hair with a honeycomb?
Can a blind bat hit a ball?
Have you ever seen a boy-footed bear?
Is a buck enough dough for a buck to purchase a doe?
Has a cat ever been accused of letting a man out of a bag?
Is a cat's paw its father?
Do cows eat milkweed?
Does the hermit crab live alone?
Does a crane have lift power?
Does a crow drink at a crowbar?
Is the cuckoo bird crazy?
If venison is expensive is it deer or dear?
Was the dinosaur sore because he couldn't soar?
If a dog can be dogmatic, can a man be manatic?
Are doghouses made out of dogwood?
Do chow dogs have 2-legs or four?
Did you know that hot dogs don't have legs?
How far could a skein fly if knotted to a skein?
Where do they find the animals for a white elephant sale?
Have you ever seen a ewe up a yew?
Can an ermine change its er mind?
Is a fish fry an offspring or a social gathering?

Herd About Town

Does a brim wear a hat?
What does it take to cause a flea to flee?
Is the fox clever enough to use the fax?
Do giraffes eat off a raffia trees?
Do greyhounds bus their young?
Does the goose ever get people bumps?
Does a ground hog own a lot of property?
Do hippocampus (seahorse) and hippopotamus share the same school?
Has a hog ever been accused of talking a lot of human-wash?
Does a horse ever get hoarse?
Do horses ever have nightmares?
Do horses nag after they get married?
Can a kite fly a kite?
Can you imagine a llama being a lama?
Have you ever seen a leopard wearing a leotard?
Have you ever heard of a human-hearted lion?
Can a lynx be a caddy on a golf links?
Does the manatee play golf underwater?
Does a mole have tunnel vision?
Isn't it the monkey's business if he throws a wrench in the works?
How come girls will scream at a mouse but will climb into a car with a wolf?
Have you ever seen a mouse with a mouse under its eye?
Do mules wear mules?
Have you ever seen a mule driving a mule?
Do mussels exercise their muscles?
Do orioles have aureoles?
Do otters wear attar?
What does the owl say when it hurts?
Do oyster spats wear spats?
Is pica the right type for a pika?
Can the pigeon speak pidgin?
Could a pigeon be a very old pig? (eon)?
Is ointment made from pigs?
Can a pike swim on a highway?
Does the porcupine come from a pig tree?
What kind of instrument is a pronghorn?
Have you ever seen a rat climb a rata tree?

Did you ever see a robin robbing a worm?
Do sardines feel like people in a subway?
Do seahorses run races?
Is it true that scallops can only move in half circles?
What would you have if a signet mated a cygnet?
Does a skate ever travel on skates?
Wouldn't it be silly to see a skimmer wearing a skimmer?
Can a secretary bird take shorthand?
Is jumbo shrimp a crustacean or an oxymoron?
Does a garter snake ever wear panty hose?
What is the exchange rate of the spoonbill?
Do stags go to parties alone?
Does the swallow have a forked tail?
Can a swallow swallow while flying?
Do swans really sing a song?
Can swans do a people dive?
Do turtle's ever wear man-necked sweaters?
Do whales have a people of a good time?
Do female whales wear lady-boned corsets?
Do whales have a people of an appetite?
Would a pack of wolves pack a suitcase for their travels?
I don't recommend a worm when fishing for a compliment.
Does a yak talk all the time?

We have seen how animals weave in and out of every aspect of our language. It would be difficult to communicate without the many ways they assist in our communication. Their participation has been effective in getting a point across. There is much to learn from the mention of animals in proverbs and literature. The wisdom of the following entries give thought to all aspects of life. It is easy to sort out the contributions of your favorite animal(s).

Proverbs

In the ants' house the dew is a flood.
Where does the ant die except in sugar?
An ant hole may collapse an embankment.
Be thine enemy an ant, see in him an elephant.

An ape is an animal with the effrontery to resemble man.

As stupid as an ass
Every ass loves to hear himself bray.
The ass loaded with gold still eats thistles.
Hay is more acceptable to an ass than gold.
No wise man stands behind an ass when he kicks.
Even if an ass goes traveling he'll not come home a horse.
An ass may bray a good while before he shakes the stars down.
I had rather ride on an ass that carries me than a horse that throws me.

As blind as a bat.

The old bear fall into the old trap.
As cross as a bear with a sore head.
Little bears have all their troubles to come.
To sell the bearskin before the bear is caught.
He must have iron nails that would scratch a bear.

To work like a beaver.
To love as the beaver does the willow.

Every bee's honey is sweet.

As nimble as a bee in a tar-barrel.
Soigné, woman, and bees, cannot be turned.
The earth is a beehive, we all enter by the same door.
What is not good for the swarm is not food for the bees.
While honey lies in every flower no doubt, it takes a bee to get the honey out.

As dull as the beetle.
One beetle recognizes another.
Every beetle is a gazelle in the eyes of its mother.

A bird's eye view.
A little bird told me.
Far birds have fair feathers.
Birds of a feather flock together.
To kill two birds with one stone.
It's an ill bird that befouls its own nest.
A bird in the hand is worth two in a bush.
If you want a bird in a cage, buy the cage first.
There are no birds of this year in last year's nest.
One swallow makes not a spring, nor a woodcock a winter
He who is not a bird should not build his nest over an abysses.
There'll be white-blackbirds before an unwilling woman ties the knot.
Though the bird may fly over your head, let it not make its nest in your hair.
A bird can roost but on one branch, a mouse can drink not more than its fill from a river.
That's the wise thrush; he sings twice over, lest you should think he never could recapture the first fine careless rapture

As hearty as a buck.

As snug as a bug in a rug.

To roar like a bull.
Like a bull in a china shop.
To take the bull by the horns.

To strut like a bullfrog.

Herd About Town

Make the calf blare and the cow will come.
Show the fattened calf but not the thing that fattened him.

A camel's kick, soft but stunning.
No camel route is long, with good company.
If the camel once gets his nose in the tent, his body will follow.

As ignorant as a cat.
A cat has nine lives.
Curiosity killed the cat.
A cat may look at a king.
To let the cat out of the bag.
A cat pent up becomes a lion.
Cats in mittens catch no mice.
A scalded cat fears cold water.
Wanton kittens make sober cats.
It's for her own good that the cat purrs.
When the cats away the mice will play.
That which comes of a cat will catch mice.
Well know the cat whose ear she licks, cats like man are flatterers.
The cats that drive the mice away are as good as they that catch them.

Harry no man's cattle.

Don't count your chickens before they are hatched.

A cock and bull story.
Cocks make free with the horse's corn.

Crow in the company of cocks.
As an old cock crows the young cock learns.

As wild as a colt.
As ragged as a colt.

As crazy as a coot.

A nimble as a cow in a cage.
A curst cow has short horns.
Milk the cow that standeth still.
Many a good cow hath a bad calf.
He that owns the cow goes nearest the tail.
Cows of many, well milked and badly fed.
Is better to kiss your cow than your enemy.
The winter the milk goes to the cow's horn.
As the old cock crows the young one learns.
A crow on the thatch, soon death lifts the latch.
Black as night the devil's kite, a carrion crow never brings luck.
The crow was always a feared and respected bird, and still today many people regard it as a bird of ill omen.

As gay as a cricket.

Crocodile tears are sincere.

A crow thinks her own bird fairest.
The crow went traveling abroad and came home just as black.
The crow does not louse the buffalo to clean him but to feed himself.

The cuckoo has but one note.

As sleek as a doe.
As swift as a deer.

A dogs life.
Dog eat dog.
As sick as a dog.
To go to the dogs.
To work like a dog.
As ashamed as a dog.
The old dog barks not in vain.
Modest dogs miss much meat.
To keep a dog and bark oneself.

Herd About Town

To be tossed like a dog in a blanket.
The slowest barker is the surest biter.
You can't teach an old dog new tricks.
A living dog is better than a dead lion.
Dogs that bark at a distance never bite.
When one dog barks another will join it.
The dog's bard, but the caravan moves on.
When the old dog barks it is time to watch.
Give a dog a bad name and it will hang him.
A dog does not always bark at the front gate
Dogs show their teeth when they dare not bite.
If you lie down with dogs you'll rise with fleas.
A dog returns to its vomit, every dog has its day.
A dog will not howl if you beat him with a bone.
He that hath nothing to spare must not keep a dog.
Who gives bread to other's dogs is often barked at by his own.
A dog in a kennel barks at his fleas; a dog hunting does not notice them.
A dog will never forget the crumb thou gavest him, though thou mayst afterwards throw a hundred stones at his head.

The dove has no gall.
As faithful as a dove.
As innocent as a dove.

The eagle soars at the sun.
An eagle will not catch flies.
An eagle's mind never fits a raven's feather.

Trumpet in a herd of elephants.

It is not fish until it is on the bank.
There are finer fish in the sea than have ever been caught.
People love goldfish because they like to see something with a mouth open that's not complaining.

A flea in one's ear.
To make a flea an elephant.

The flea though he kill none, he does all the harm he can.
A reasonable amount of fleas is good for dog, it keeps him from brooding.
Great fleas have little fleas upon their backs to bite 'em and little fleas have lesser fleas, and so on ad infinitum.

A fly in the ointment.
A fly may disturb the sleeping lion.
To skin a flea for its hide and tallow
Who lies with dogs shall rise up with fleas.
Do nothing hastily but the catching of fleas.
Don't imitate the fly before you have wings.
A fly may sting a horse and make him wince.
More flies are caught with honey, than with vinegar.
The fly ought to be used as the symbol of impertinence and audacity, for whilst all other animals shun man more than anything else, and run away before he come near them, the fly lights right upon his very nose!

As sly as a fox.
As cunning as a fox
Old foxes want no tutors.
Foxes dig not their own holes.
An old fox need learn no craft.
An old fox understands the trap.
The tail doth often catch the fox.
With foxes we must play the fox.
The fox condemns the trap, not himself.
The fox may grow grey but never good.
When the fox preaches, beware the geese.
Every fox must pay his own skin to the flayer.
He that will get the better of a fox must rise early.
A wise fox will never rob his neighbor's henhouse.
The wiles of the fox will never enter the lion's head.
The fox knows much, but more he that catcheth him.
The fox never found a better messenger than himself
A foolish fox is caught by one leg but, a wise one by all four.

Herd About Town

As cold as a frog.
Like a frog upon a gridiron.
Like frogs after a heavy rain.

All one's geese are swans.

Bleat in a flock of goats.
The lust of the goat is the bounty of God.
It is difficult to choose between two blind goats.
Do not mistake a goats beard for a fine stallion's tail.

As dizzy as a goose.
A wild goose chase.
A wild goose never reared a tame gosling.
To kill the goose that lays the golden eggs.
What's food for the goose is good for the gander.

As mad as a March hare.
Don't hunt two hares with one dog.
Even the hare will insult a dead lion.
Hares can gambol over the body of a dead lion.
To run with the hare and hunt with the hounds.

To watch like a hawk.
You tell a hawk from a hand saw.
To be between hawk and buzzard.

Mad as a wet hen.
As busy as a hen with one chick.
It's a bad hen that won't scratch herself.

As fat as a hog.
As nasty as hogs.
To go whole hog.
Hogs see the wind.
A hog will run forward.
To run like a scolded hog.

A hog on trust grunts till he's paid.
A hog swimming cuts its own throat.
No hog can trespass on his masters ground.

As fierce as a hornet.

A horse laugh.
To snort like a horse.
To work like a horse.
A horse of another color.
A galled horse will wince.
To ride a free horse to death.
Trouble rides fast on a horse.
Water trotted is as good as oats.
Win the horse or lose the saddle.
Nothing so bold as a blind mare.
All lay load on the willing horse.
A hired horse a tired horse never.
One cannot shoe a running horse.
Don't judge a horse by the harness.
Nothing is so bold as a blind mare.
One saddle is enough for one horse.
Good horses can't be of a bad color.
Don't look a gift horse in the mouth
Live horse and thou shall get grass.
Good horses can't be of a bad color.
A horse taught and a woman to teach.
He that leads his horse may well go a foot.
The old horse must die in someone's keeping.
Trust neither a horse's heel nor a dog's tooth.
A dapple-grey horse will sooner die than tire.
Happiness is not a horse, you cannot harness it.
If two men ride a horse, one must ride behind.
The old horse may die waiting for the new grass.
Let a horse drink when he will, not what he will.
The stable wears out a horse more than the road.
Who has a good horse in his stable can go a foot.

Herd About Town

Though you ride, remember the horse goes on foot.
It is a bad horse that will not carry his own provender.
One man may better steal a horse than another look on.
A cough will stick longer by a horse than a peck of oats.
The buyer needs a hundred eyes, the horse thief not one.
If you meet a piebald horse, wish before you see his tail.
A horse thinks one thing, and he that saddles him another.
The man who does not love a horse cannot love a woman.
A statement once let loose cannot be caught by four horses.
Have a horse of thine own and thou mayst borrow another's.
One may lead a horse to water but, he can't make him drink it.
The horses of hope gallop, but the asses of experience go slowly.
He that hath a white horse and a fair wife need never want for trouble.
In buying a horse and taking a wife, shut your eyes and commend yourself to God.
In selling a horse praise his bad points, and leave the good ones to look after themselves.

.As white as a hounds tooth.

As light as a hummingbird.

To cut off the hyena's head.

As yellow as a kite's foot.

As pure as a lamb.
As gentle as lambs.
A pet lamb makes a cross ram.
May as well be hanged for a sheep as a lamb.

A blithe as a lark.
As cherry as a lark.
To rise with the lark.
A lark is worth a kite.
When the sky falls we all catch larks.

To beard the lion.
To roar like a lion.
As brave as a lion.
Wake not the sleeping lion.
Lions in peace, deer in war.
To throw at the lion with corks.
You can tell the lion by his paw.
If the lion says the lamb is a fox, it must be so.
If one plays with the lion, let him beware of his paw.
If the lion's skin will not do, we must sew on that of the fox.
He that has gone so far a s to cut the claws of a lion, will not feel himself secure until he has drawn his teeth.

Can the Ethiopian change his skin, or the leopard his spots.
Rain beats a leopard's skin, but it does not wash off the spots.

A lizard on a cushion will still seek leaves.

To have a lynx's eye.

As the maggot bites.
To have maggots in the brain.

As greedy as a magpie.
To chatter like a magpie.

Lean as a mink.

Burn not your house to fright away the mice.

To grin like a monkey.
As nimble as a monkey.
As mischievous as a monkey.
The higher a monkey climbs the more we see his tail.

As lean as a mouse.
A silent as a mouse.

Herd About Town

As poor as a church mouse.
A mouse can build a home with out timber.
The mouse by diligence bit in two the cable.
Better a mouse in the pot than no flesh at all.
It is a bold mouse that nestles in the cat's ear.
Not the mouse is the thief, but the hole in the wall.
When the mouse laughs at the cat there is a hole nearby.
In baiting a mousetrap with cheese, always leave room for the mouse.

As stubborn as a mule.

To play opossum.

The ostrich hides its head.

As grave as an owl.
An owl in an ivy bush.
The owl is the king of the night.
The owl is the Welshman's nightingale.
He greatly needs a bird that gives a goat to an owl.

As big as an ox.
As patient as oxen
An old ox ploughs a straight furrow.
Muzzle not the ox that treads the corn.
An old ox will find shelter for himself.
When the ox stumbles, all whet their knaves.
An ox remains an oz, even if driven to Vienna.
A man must plough with such oxen as he hath.
The stolen ox sometimes puts his head out of the stall.
One hair of a woman draws more than a team of oxen.
An ox with long horns, even if he does not butt, will be accused of butting.

As happy as oysters.
As passive as oysters.
Not worth an oysters shell.

As plump as a partridge.

As proud as a peacock.
A peacock has gay feathers but, black feet.
No peacock envies another peacock his tail.

Pigs might fly, but they are most unlikely birds.
Pigs grow fat where lambs would starve.
A pretty pig makes an ugly sow.
A pig that has two owners is sure to die of hunger.
Never give cherries to a pig or advice to a fool.

As stupid as a pig.
In a pig's whisper.
To bleed like a pig.
As drunk as a sow.
To sleep like a pig.
To squeal like a pig.
Pigs play upon organs.
To buy a pig in a poke.
To roar like a stuck pig.
To let the pig out of the bag.
To have the wrong pig by the ear.
Pigs that sleep together become fond.

To coo like pigeons.
To send one for pigeon milk.
Roasted pigeons will not fly into one's mouth.
When pigeons go a benting, the farmers go lamenting.

To breed like rabbits.
A rabbit is fat three days in the week.
A tyro woman will never buy a rabbit without a head for fear it's a cat.

To pay with a ram skin.
To ploy with a ram's horn.

Herd About Town

To smell a rat.
As dead as a rat.
As poor as a rat.
As weak as a rat.
One rat brings another.
As wet as a drowned rat.
Rats abandon a sinking ship.
Rats flee from a falling house.
A rat that has but one hole (is in danger).

To the raven her own chicks are white.
He that takes the raven for his guide will light on carrion.

As black as a raven.
Raise ravens and they will peck out your eyes.

He that hurts a robin will never prosper.
If you touch a robin's nest you will have a crooked finger all your life.

As swift as a roe.

As greedy as sharks.
As hungry as a shark.
As voracious as a shark.

To follow like sheep.
To die like rotten sheep.
There is a black sheep in every flock.
One foolish sheep will lead the flock.
The wool seller knows the wool buyer.
As well be hanged for a sheep as a lamb.
Shear your sheep when elder blossoms peep.
Many go out for wool and come home shorn.
You were better given the wool than the sheep.
He that makes himself a sheep the wolves will eat.
It is a foolish sheep that makes a wolf its confessor.
He that has one sheep in the flock will like all the rest the better for it.

To keep like sheep in fold, there was never a scabby sheep in a flock that didn't like to have a comrade.

At a snail's pace.
Tread on a snail and it will turn.
A snail has everything on its back.

As poor as a snake.
A snake in the grass.
As smooth as a snake.

Sparrows who emulate peacocks are likely to break a thigh.
The sparrow is sorry for the peacock at the burden of its tail.

When spider's webs unite, they can tie up a lion.
If you wish to live and thrive, let a spider run alive.

As white as a swan.
The swan sings before its death.

He who rides the tiger can never dismount.
Those who hunt deer sometimes raise tigers.
Unless you enter the tiger's den you cannot take the cubs.
Do not blame God for having created the tiger, but thank him for not having given it wings.

A toad under a hallow.
As full as a toad of poison.

As true as a trout.
There's no catching trout with dry breeches.

A turkey never voted for an early Thanksgiving or Christmas.

As fractious as a wasp.

As lank as a weasel

Herd About Town

As thick as weasels.

To skulk lie wolves.
Man is wolf to man.
As ragged as wolves.
A wolf in sheep's clothing.
To keep the wolf from the door.
The wolf knows what the ill beast thinks.
The wolf changes his coat but not his nature.
The wolf loses his teeth, but not his inclinations.
No matter how much you feed a wolf he will always return to the forest.

Tread on a worm and it will turn.

Quotes

The role of animals in our language is given credibility through some of our greatest thinkers. Evidence animals have not been overlooked by the giants of literature is presented below.

I think I could turn and live with animals, they are so placid and self-contained, I stand and look at them long and long they do not sweat and whine about their condition, they do not lie awake in the darkness and weep for their sins.
Walt Whitman

The behavior of men, to the lower animals and their behavior to each other, bear a constant relationship.
Herbert Spencer

As a thinker and planner the ant is the equal of any savage race of men; as a self-educated specialist in several arts she is the superior of any savage race of men; and in one or two high mental qualities she is above the reach of any man, savage or civilized.
Mark Twain

The behavior of men, to the lower animals and their behavior to each other, bear a constant relationship.
Herbert Spencer

Ant and savages put strangers to death.
Bertrand Russell

I must dance barefoot on her wedding day and, for your love for her, lead apes in hell.

Shakespeare

I am a bear of very little brain, and long words bother me.

Winnie the Pooh

It is not only fine feathers that make fine birds.

Aesop

No bird soars too high if he soars with his own wings.

Blake

Should you read, upon an enclosure with an elephant, a sign saying buffalo, believe not your eyes.

Tolstoy

In time the savage bull does bear the yoke.

Shakespeare

Haven't your sometimes seen a cloud that looked like a centaur? Or a leopard perhaps? Or a wolf? Or a bull?

Aristophanes

Sherman's buzzing' along to de sea like Moses ridin' on a bumblebee.

Benet

Thou wear a lion's hide! Doff it for shame, and hang a calf's-skin on those recreant limbs.

Shakespeare

Those who'll play with cats must expect to be scratched.

Cervantes

The cat in gloves catches no mice.

Franklin

But thousands die, without or this or that. Die, and endow a college, or a cat.

Pope

Keep no more cats than will catch mice.
Cervantes

There are more ways of killing a cat than choking her with cream.
Kingsley

Man scans with scrupulous care the character and pedigree of his horses, cattle, and dogs before he matches them; but when he comes to his own marriage he rarely, or never, takes any such care.
Darwin

Do not count your chickens before they are hatched.
Aesop

Like cicadas, which sit upon a tree in the forest and pour out their piping voices, so the leaders of Trojans were sitting on the tower.
Homer

A cock has great influence on his own dunghill.
Syrus

The public buys its opinions as it buys its meat, or takes in its milk, on the principle that it is cheaper to do this than to keep a cow. So it is, but the milk is more likely to be watered.
Butler

Kiss till the cows come home.
Fletcher

You cannot teach a crab to walk straight.
Aristophanes

They say a reasonable number of fleas is good for a dog--keeps him from brooding over being 'a dog.
Westcott

A dog is the only thing on earth that loves you more than he loves himself.
Josh Billings

He that lies with the dogs, riseth with fleas.
Herbert

Whoever beats dogs loves not man.
Arsene Houssaye

You pick up a starving dog and make him prosperous he will not bite you. This is the principal difference between a dog and a man.
Mark Twain

The dove loves when it quarrels; the wolf hates when it flatters.
St. Augustine

I wish the bald eagle had not been chosen as the representative of our country; he is a bird of bad moral character; like those among men who live by sharping and robbing, he is generally poor, and often very lousy.
Franklin

Extract yourself from bad ways like an elephant stuck in the mud.
Suttapitaka

Should you read, upon an enclosure with an elephant, a sign saying buffalo, believe not your eyes.
Tolstoy

The flea, though he kills none, he does all the harm he can.
Donne

I'd sooner, except the penalties, kill a man than a hawk.
Jeffers

A hen is only an egg's way of making another egg.

Butler

The sun has a right to "set" where it wants to, and so, I might add has a hen.
Browne

In the choice of a horse and a wife, a man must please himself, ignoring the opinion and advice of friends.
Whyte-Melville

A little neglect may breed great mischief, for want of a nail the shoe was lost; for want of a shoe the horse was lost; and for want of a horse the rider was lost.
Franklin

It is nought good a sleeping hound to wake.
Chaucer

God tempers the wind to the shorn lamb.
Estienne

Like the lark that soars in the air, first singing, then silent, content with the last sweetness that satiates it, such seemed to me that image, the imprint of the Eternal Pleasure.
William of Ockham

Death is afraid of him because he has the heart of a lion.
Arab Proverb

To bring in god shield us! A lion among ladies, is a most dreadful thing, for there is not a more fearful wild-fowl than your lion living.
Shakespeare

When a building is about to fall down, all the mice desert it.
Pliny the Elder

I believe that our Heavenly Father invented man because he was disappointed in the monkey.
Aldrich

Consider the little mouse, how sagacious an animal it is which never entrusts its life to one hole only.
Plautus

Darwinian Man, though well-behaved, at best is only a monkey shaved.
Gilbert

Consider the little mouse, how sagacious an animal it is which never entrusts its life to one hole only.
Plautus

The tired ox treads with a firmer step.
St. Jerome

This man of little learning grows old like an ox: his flesh increases, but not his wisdom.
Suttapitaka

The pride of the peacock is the glory of God.
Blake

I began to smell a rat. The proof of the pudding is in the eating.
Cervantes

Take care! Kingdoms are destroyed by bandits, houses, by rats, and widows by suitors.
Saikaku

Laws are like spiders' webs, which stand firm when any light, yielding object falls upon them, while a larger thing breaks through them and escapes.
Solon

One swallow does not make a summer.
Aristotle

The tadpole poet will never grow into anything bigger than a frog; not though in that stage of development he should puff and blow himself till he bursts with windy adulation at the heels of the lauded ox.

Swineburne

We end this chapter giving rhyming credence to the way animals communicate among themselves. We need to be careful to not fall into to the grunt and groan approach ourselves.

Barnyard Onomatopoeia

Their formation an imitation of sound
Descriptive words not necessarily profound
Enhancing the rhetorical value of speech
A special meaning to those they reach

This verse attempts to explain
It's to use with an animal's name
The wolf of the dog and its bow wow
The kitten purring and the cats meow

Chickens cluck and chicks peep
Harmonizing with the baa-ing sheep
A rooster does his cock-a-doddlle-doo
And cows utter their mournful moo

Turkey's walk about in a wobble
Vocalizing their tune of gobble
Horses communicate with a neigh
Donkeys chime in with a bray

The hummingbird swishes from a tree
In competition with the buzzing bee
Peacocks strut about proudly
Pigs contempt is heard loudly

A farm sure has its grunts and snorts
Whispers, snarls and howls of all sorts
Where grown is preferred to groan
You'll never feel alone

The song of the hawk
Is more like a squawk
The antics of the flicker
Often brings a snicker

Coyotes sing a mournful cry
Geese fill the cloudless sky
The plow moves with a clatter
Sending the earth in a splatter

Humans also use grunts and groan
It's not for animals alone

Superstitions and Myths

Everyone at some period in their lives has experienced a sense of insecurity. The world around becomes threatening, certainties dissolve into uncertainties; suddenly we become afraid. This is not necessarily an irrational attitude: it is often our moment of truth.

Only then are we face to face with what some people might call reality, a truth so overwhelming that it seems to threaten sanity itself. It is at this time that we turn away from the world we know to those secret powers or spirits which our ancestors believed waited at the side of every individual under duress to see him through crisis. We perform little secret rites that we feel may somehow counter the blows of fate, or at least offset imaginary disasters. These rituals we call superstitions, but to an earlier generation they were known as magic.

The word superstition is derived from the Latin word *super*; above, and *stare*: to stand. In ancient times those who survived in battle were called superstitions because they had outlived their opponents. Our modern superstitions fall into this class for they so often represent bizarre modes of thought that survived the ages which created them, to linger on in our midst like ghosts from an unknown past.

Basically, superstition and all that it involves is concerned with specific attitudes towards the world of spirits. At the root of most of our surviving superstition lies an implicit acceptance of magic as a rule of life, which in effect means the possibility of control by man over his destiny by the exercise of rituals to which the forces governing the external world have no option but to submit.

Animals have inspired and continue to play an important role in defining superstition. Most of us are familiar with the claim that bad luck will come your way if a black cat crosses your path or walks toward you. Getting the long end of breaking of the wish-bone of the chicken or carrying a rabbits foot for good luck have been long accepted tales. If they have worked for you, you may want to try some of the ones listed below. For sure, some you will want to avoid. The selection of superstitions, centering on animals, leaves some doubt of the validity of it all; review them with an inquiring eye.

To kill an albatross is to bring ill luck to the ship and all upon it. The albatross is the largest of the seabirds which follow ships out to sea. It is often the last bird left flying with the ship to the final tie to shore. Sailors have watched albatross closely, thought about them often, and turned these thoughts into stories and superstitions.

Some say that each albatross is the soul of a drowned sailor who follows the ship to be close to his mates. Other stories tell of an albatross, which is very strong, lifting shipwrecked sailors out of the sea and carrying them safely to shore. Certainly, it would be bad luck to kill a bird that had the soul of a shipmate or that might save your life.

Many believe that destroying an anthill will bring bad luck. Others interpret dreams involving ants mean some impending frustration. If you have any doubt you can remove ants from a house by taking some of them to a neighbor on a leaf and the others will follow. Some claim to get rid of ants involves only the use of chalk, drawing a circle round the area you want to protect. Be aware some ants will cross a chalk mark.

Bats are birds (actually mammals) of both good and bad omens. They are "witches" to some. To others they denote happiness, peace, long life, wealth and virtue. There is a popular belief that the devil, when he isn't doing something to bother people, takes the shape of a bat. Some believe that the bat is a familiar (the servant of a witch). Closely aligned is the belief that ghosts take the form of bats and therefore houses with bats in them are haunted.

Another superstition, that many believe, is that if you wash your face in the blood of a bat, you will be able to see in the dark. Watch out if a bat lands on your head, it will not leave until it hears the thunder of an approaching rainstorm.

Finally, here is the good side. To the Chinese and the Poles, bats are a good omen. The Chinese say that bats fly with their bodies down because their brains are so heavy and also believe that the bat is the symbol of long life and happiness.

The bee's sting is mentioned in several superstitions: bees can't sting you while you are holding your breath, they can only sting once, and before cutting down a tree with bees in it you only need to say certain magic words and they will not sting. Beating pans, ringing cow bells or making noise generally, is supposed to scare swarming bees and induce them to settle down, but it is unlikely bees hear sounds.

Some African-Americans are highly superstitious when it comes to bees. For example, bees seen in swarms foretell death; a bee sting means a betrayal; a dream about bees making honey is a sign of honor; a dream about killing a bee suggests some forthcoming loss. It is risky to sell a beehive without further ritual. A bee sale should be accompanied with another corresponding transaction of value (such as a bushel of corn).

In western Pennsylvania some say that bees single out red-headed persons, overlook idiots and people with good dispositions.

A yellow honey bee flying around a person is a sign of forthcoming good news; if it is black, beware of bad news. If a bee flies into a window it is an omen of good news and is the souls of departed people and they are in close contact with spirits and gods. It is also common confidence that a bee ignored will not sting (unfortunately not true).

The relationship between humans and birds is special. Ancient societies in some places revered them. It was believed that birds could talk and that certain people could understand them. When a wise man learned to imitate birds he could inform a gullible audience that "a little bird told me" whenever his wisdom was questioned.

Some claim that an encounter with a mad bull will bring safety if you look it squarely in the eye; it will not charge you. The saying goes: "look me straight in the eyes" when a lie is suspected. (This is also a poor test since a good liar never reveals his lying.) It is also not recommended to take the charging bull superstition literally.

It is generally thought that butterflies bring good luck. If the first butterfly you see in the year is white, you will have good luck all year. Three butterflies together also mean good luck. A third speculation is a little harder to take advantage of-if you bite the head off of the first butterfly you see in a year, you will have good luck all year.

Canaries are also subjects of superstitions both good and bad. A strange canary flying into a house spells death to a member of the family. A strange cat which kills a pet canary means bad luck for two years. Others believe pet canaries bring harmony to a home. Better to keep the cat away.

Egyptians had a cat god, Bast. She was the goddess of pleasure and protected men against contagious disease and other evils. In Bast's honor, they mummified cats. Black cats were also considered a lucky symbol by the

Egyptians.

The ancient Hebrews believed the ashes of a black kitten would enable one to see demons. Today people are afraid when a black cat crosses their path. The story changes depending where you are; in Britain it's unlucky to say the word cat while you're down in a mine, in Texas they say you're in luck if a black cat comes into your house, provided it stays, in Lancashire, it's unlucky if a cat dies in your house (certainly for the cat).

In Azande of Africa, some women are supposed to give birth to cats; nobody can deny this, for to see one of them is to die. Chinese emperors slept on cat-shaped pillows for luck. Buddhists will tell you where cats come from. A rat ate part of one of Buddha's scriptures, so the Enlightened One rubbed a little skin off the inside of his arm and from that made the first cat. The proof, rats are still afraid of cats.

Superstitions get a bit confusing with cats. It' good luck if a strange cat visits your home, but bad luck if it decides to stay. It's bad luck to carry a cat into a house or to have your picture taken with a cat. Yet if the cat of your house is black, of lovers you will not lack. In Texas the theory is altered to the belief that you're in luck if a black cat comes into your house, provided it stays.

At times the cat stories border on the ridiculous. For instance, cats born in the month of May cannot catch rats or mice. A cat will stay at home if you butter its paws. If a man accidentally steps on a cat's tail he will marry before the year is out.

A more serious message comes from Cicadas. When they are in a horde, it's said to be a sign of an approaching war. It is the "w" shaped marking on the wings which has led to this meaning. On the bright side, contrary to common opinion the cicada's sting will not kill a person.

Most are familiar with the theory, the breaking of a wish-bone of a chicken or turkey is a sign of good luck and fulfilled wish to the one who gets the long end of the break. Lesser-known is the legend that says the crow was originally white but he turned black after eating snake eyes.

A single crow cawing near a house is an omen of approaching calamity. The first crow seen in the spring in flight means that one will be taking a trip. Seeing a crow in flight is the time to make a wish; if it continues in flight without flapping its wings the wish will come true; if it flaps its wings, one should look away to have their wish fulfilled. A crow in flight to the left means bad news; if flying on the right this means to be on one's guard for the day.

To save yourself from the bad luck which comes from seeing just one crow, bow your head until the bird has gone. If you have a hat on, take it off. Crows are not as easily scared as the widespread belief in scare-crows indicates. A scare-crow is probably the outgrowth of the idea of the protection of a cross against intruders and evil spirits. Part of the effectiveness of scare-crows is due to the odor of man which birds may scent.

A cow will not mourn the loss of its calf taken from her if the calf is taken out of the barn backward. To find a lost cow, catch a grandpa's long-legs, place a finger on one leg and it will point the other leg in the direction in which the cow may be found. Can't we get more fun than that from grandpas?

Crickets foretell weather, warn of death, foretell good or bad luck, and tell of the approach of friends. If crickets come into a house they bring good luck but it is not good to kill a cricket (especially on Sunday). There is a school of thought that believes carrying a cricket's nest with you is good luck.

Man's best friend hasn't escaped the superstitions. Ghostly dogs protect long-dead people, demon dogs accompany witches, headless dogs run rampant in legend, and even real dogs are involved in superstitions. Many Egyptians since ancient times have believed dogs to have a kind of ESP.

Dogs were often regarded as the familiar spirits of witches and wizards. They were considered to be emissaries of the Devil in animal form, bestowed upon their earthly masters to do their bidding. Some of the developments include-if a yellow dog happens to follow on one's tracks this is an omen of good luck. A strange dog following on one's heels or making its home with you also brings good luck. Dogs know whether or not a person can be trusted. If a dog passes between a man and a woman who are going to be married, the marriage will have ill luck. If a dog howls at night, particularly at the moon, this means death.

There is more! Some are convinced if you and your dog share the same pillow, you will also share the same dream, and others claim you must snap your fingers at the same time you whistle for a dog-otherwise you would whistle up the devil as well as the dog.

The dove is the symbol of the Holy Spirit (often suspended over a pulpit where the Word of God is believed to be proclaimed). White doves nesting in the beams of one's house are considered good luck by many Islamics. Ali, son-in-law and cousin of Mohammed, used to wish his friends the blessing of white doves. He is reputedly buried in a mosque in Afghanistan, where, it is said; flocks of white pigeons have guarded his tomb for centuries. It is certainly true that if a pigeon with black feathers in its plumage tries to roost there, the white ones drive it violently away.

Some contend that eagles carry off lambs and children (an unfounded superstition). There is an ancient Egyptian belief that every ten years the eagle soars through the fires of Hell and then sheds its feathers, thereby acquiring a new life. There is another ancient legend that Adam and Eve didn't die but were actually turned into eagles and went to live on an island off the coast of Ireland (any guesses who thought that one up?).

Through the centuries the eagle has come to stand for strength and swiftness, and it was the emblem of many royal houses and, of course, our national symbol. The Romans began using the double-headed eagle when their empire merged with the Germans', joining their eagle to that of the Huns .In folklore the eagle has always been a helpful bird, bringing warnings of trouble to the heroes.

It is a common belief that dreaming about flies foretells sickness. If many flies get into a house this, too, is a warning that sickness is coming. Flying around the country, we find in Kentucky and Louisiana heraldry that a fly buzzing around a person persistently is a sign of someone desiring to see the individual. To kill this fly means assurance of this meeting. In New England, it was common belief that dragon flies were capable of sewing up various parts of the body, such as eyelids, ears, lips, and nostrils. In Iowa, the superstition holds that exposed fingers or toes would be sewed together by a visiting dragonfly.

A firefly is often called a "lightning bug." Be sure to count the number if either get into your house, if one it is an omen of one person less or one person more in the house on the following day. Two fire flies in a house mean that there will be a marriage of the unmarried in the household. A large number of fireflies in the house are an omen of good company coming.

For some, a firefly means death to an occupant of a house unless it is captured and confined in a glass until its death.

Fishermen are known for their exaggerated tales. They also have superstitions such as refusing to ship out on Friday until one minute past midnight. If a captain invites some friend aboard and the boatmen do not catch fish the boat is headed for shore and the guest is politely dismissed.

Watch out for these tales before you throw in a line. Telling a companion of a fish on the line before it is landed will mean failure to land it. Catch a fish on the first cast and there will be no further bites (some fishermen throw back the first fish of the season, for luck). A fish caught and not wanted should be kept and not be thrown back into the water until you have finished fishing.

Otherwise, your unwanted fish will communicate to others and warn them away from your hook. If you count the number of fish you have caught, you will catch no more that day. A fish should always be eaten from the head towards the tail.

Fish are a symbol of life, fishing is a sign of peaceful life, and to see a fish in the water is to receive unexpected favors. Most dreams of fish are said to forecast good luck but a dead fish means loss, and cleaning and dressing a mackerel stands for deceit and evil tidings.

Sun cured fish, a favorite article of diet, is used in many folk ideas and customs. A superstition associated with salt fish forecasts if a "dream line" (strip in the center) is eaten before going to bed a girl or young man would see in a vision of the person who is to become her or his marital partner handing out a glass of water.

To see one fox is lucky but be careful to avoid a brace of fox. To see many is unlucky. Also be aware the bark of a fox presages death.

Since ancient times the frog was held to be an important symbol of inspiration and of fertility (due to the large number of eggs it lays at one time). The frog was so important in that time that when one died in Egypt it was embalmed. It was also popular as a Roman mascot and is still believed to be very good luck in the home.

Some people in Korea say that if you see a frog that has red eyes, you'll have bad luck. But others in the southern United States have a saying that it's very lucky to see any frog. It means you're going to get money!

Frogs should be handled with care to avoid the belief of some that if you kill a frog the cow will give bloody milk. Others contend what you are doing when in the spring you hear the first frog, this same thing you will be doing much of the year.

Even today the frog is considered a fairly reliable weatherman because of its susceptibility to atmospheric changes, which cause it to croak whenever the barometer goes down. We now close our coats with frogs (an ornamental cloth consisting of a button and a loop through which it passes), perhaps a holdover from an early French custom where frogs were embroidered on to clothes for good luck.

Roost goose for dinner on St. Michael's day is an English tradition comparable to turkey at Thanksgiving in America. It has the distinction of bringing good fortune throughout the year.

The idea has long persisted that if a ground hog sees his shadow on

February 2 at high noon he will crawl back to his winter hibernation for another six weeks, thus predicting a delayed spring. If he does not see his shadow he will not return to his burrow, thus foreshadowing an early spring. You shouldn't depend on this for planting your early garden.

A hawk is an omen of victory or success when seen flying overhead, in the act of decision or in a contest engaged by the observer. A hawk's skin is a lucky charm but if a hawk lands on the rigging of a ship it brings bad luck.

When the mane of a horse gets tangled this is an indication that some witch has been there and tied a knot to make for itself a stirrup. If, in a stable, a horse shows signs of sweating this suggests that it has been ridden by a witch.

If a horse lies down and rolls over, the number of times it rolls indicates its worth; each complete roll equals one hundred dollars. On many farms in America it is held that if one buys a horse and changes its name this will bring bad luck with it.

A gray horse is the omen of good luck. If one spits on the little finger and rubs it on the horse there will be money in the offering. A white horse may bring bad luck unless the person spits in its direction. A Hungarian tradition holds that one is more likely to enjoy success if one is mounted on a black horse than upon on of any other color.

Horsemen in general, hold a mortal dread of taking thirteen horses to a meeting. They are sensitive to such simple things as a hat on a bed, and inverted horseshoe over a door, the creaking of a door or the tap of a beetle's head. Yet many believe a horse-hair lariat laid down around a blanket will keep snakes from entering your immediate vicinity, protecting you while you sleep. See discussion under snake myths below.

The reason a horse blows on water before drinking at night is that water sometimes sleeps, and if an animal were to drink sleeping water, it would die. Blowing wakes the water up. A horse-hair kept in warm water will become a snake. A horseshoe is a good luck sign.

More than seven spots on the wing-cover of a lady bug is an omen of famine but less than seven foretells of a good harvest. Generally, a ladybug will bring money but it is bad luck to kill one.

A typical American saying known among children is "Ladybug Ladybug, fly away from home, your house is on fire and your children will burn." One is then supposed to ask questions to the captured ladybug and make wishes for good luck. "Plenty of ladybugs, plenty of hops" is a phrase of charm and good luck to many farmers. If a ladybug lights on a person it will bring good luck.

When making a wish with a ladybug in the hand, the direction it goes in flight will indicate from where the good luck will come. This is "true" particularly to a lady hopeful of marriage; she will then know the direction from which her groom will appear.

March comes in like a lamb it goes out like a lion and a black lamb means good luck for the flock are well-known, but to dream of a lizard is a sign that you have a secret enemy doesn't hold the same popularity. Also, a marriage will not be happy if a lizard crosses the path of the wedding party is not held in high esteem. A black lamb means good luck for the flock and it is considered good luck for us.

The owl was the constant companion of Athena, the Greek goddess of wisdom. Because Athens was her city, the owl was sacred in the city, and Athena was almost overrun by them. The Romans, on the other hand, hated the owl considering it a bad omen and believing its hooting meant death.

Today it is believed that the owl can foretell the future and if one hoots or hollers near your house disaster is not too far off. It may even be foretelling a death in the family. So wear your clothes backward, pull out your pockets, throw salt over your left shoulder, and put a knot in your handkerchief to avoid these fates.

The American Indians believed that an owl signaled approaching death. Another owl tale of ill fortune persists that an owl perched on a house predicts death to an occupant, thus "death's dreadful messenger." In Wales the hoot of an owl was the sign of an unmarried girl's surrender of her chastity.

It is bad luck to see an owl in the sunlight and if an owl lands on the rigging of a ship it brings bad luck. For a change of pace students carry owl charms to bring them good luck in examinations believing it is the "bird of wisdom."

The oyster is alleged to be one of nature's true aphrodisiacs. Along the lines of the ancient belief that like makes like, it was thought that the oyster, which resembles the female reproductive organs, would stimulate sexual aid. Lord Byron in "Don Juan"11 said, "Oysters are amatory food."

The idea that oysters are unwholesome in all months that have not an "r" is suspect. During those months oysters lay their eggs. It makes more sense to avoid them when the lack of refrigeration doubled the spoilage rate of oysters in those months.

Theatrical people once shied away from wearing peacock feathers as harbingers of bad luck. The reverse is now true: they are good luck charms in the American theater, although receiving mixed reviews elsewhere. It's different with the cry of a peacock under a window which is believed to signal the death of an occupant of the house.

Since the earliest recorded times, the peacock has been highly esteemed in China and Japan. It was an indication of rank and a reward for achievement from the rulers. In India, the peacock was lucky because it warned of approaching evil, and it was thought to be magical. The Indians say the peacock "has an angel's feathers, a devil's voice and a thief's walk." In the sixteenth century, peacock feathers were bestowed upon liars and cheats to signify they were traitors

It is bad to kill a pig, when the moon is waning. The flesh may not take salt (and consequently won't cure), and the bacon will shrink in the pan. It is an old Scottish tradition that pigs and parsons on board ship bring bad luck to fishermen. Others worry if pigs run off; it warns of sickness coming to the family.

The natives of Sumatra save the jawbones of the pigs they have eaten and suspend them from the ceiling. This is thought to guarantee the salvation of each little porker's soul. Many people in the south of the United States hold the superstitious belief that the eating of pig-jowls and black eyed peas on New Year's Day will bring good luck throughout the year. Also if you have a run of bad luck and wish to break it, pull a pig's tail.

The praying mantis is an insect regarded by many as a symbol of holiness and therefore bad luck comes to him who kills it. Its "holiness" rests on the suggestion arising from its observed posture which is that of clasped front legs. If it seems to kneel down to him who observes it there will come a vision of an angel.

In the southern United States the mantis is called an agent of the devil. It should be left alone. It is very bad luck to kill one plus there is a twenty-five dollar fine for harming one. If a praying mantis alights on one's hand one will meet a distinguished person; if it lands on the head one will shortly receive some great honor. If it injures one, they will lose a valued friend.

Carrying a rabbit's foot has long thought to be good luck. It all started because of the unusual way the rabbit runs. The strong hind legs touch the ground ahead of its front ones (a most unusual way for an animal to walk). This led ancients who thought the technique so remarkable to ascribe magical powers to those feet.

If a rabbit crosses the road behind you, it is good luck but, if one crosses in front of you, it could mean problems. To avoid trouble cross yourself, or make an "x" in the road, spit on it, and walk backward over it before continuing on your way.

Rats are perhaps the most famous as foretellers of maritime disaster. Rats leaving a sinking ship are a classic symbol of escape from falling fortune. It works at home as well. Rats leaving one house for another are said to bring bad luck to those who live in the house from which they left and good luck to those in residence in the house they have entered. If you would rather not participate know that rats will not go through a soaped hole or if you catch one and paint it and then let it loose. When the rats see this strange creature they will flee the area.

Superstition connects rats and teeth in many parts of the world because rats' teeth are so strong. A common superstition is one in which a child's milk tooth is thrown into the grass with a charm where rats nest asking the rats to accept the tooth and to give a strong one in return.

A robin is an omen of both good and bad luck. A robin's nest near one's house is an omen of good luck but that would change if the nest is neither injured nor disturbed. A robin held prisoner in the house brings bad luck. A robin appearing in the morning is the sign of a visitor coming on the same day.

Many myths exist concerning snakes. That snakes travel in pairs is unfounded. Usually snakes inhabit specific vicinity, but do not move about in pairs. Thus, the killing of a snake is said to bring on the revenge of its partner is a superstition to go the baseless ones that follow. You might kill a snake, but no matter how many pieces you cut it into, it would not die before the sun went down. If you try to kill a snake after dark, it will not die. Dreaming of snakes is an omen that you have an enemy. Killing the snake in this dream means you will outsmart this enemy. You can keep your youth by eating one snake a month at the time of the full moon.

Spiders are popular in superstitions. If a spider approaches this is a sign of a letter is coming. A spider in the morning is a sign of sorrow; a spider at noon brings worry for tomorrow; a spider in the afternoon is a sign of a gift; but a spider in the evening will all hopes uplift. To kill a spider is to bring rain or poverty; it also brings bad luck. If you find a spider on your clothes you can expect to get some money very soon. But if someone else found a spider on your clothes you would expect to lose money soon.

Centuries ago there was already a belief that a stork flies over a house where a birth is about to take place. It's a small step from that to the legend of the stork as the bringer of babies and of good luck that expands to that it brings many children and good luck to the family living in the house where it makes its nest.

The stork bird is also a symbol of protection. So valued are storks as symbols of domestic bliss-for which their habit of mating for life provides a good example-that when these birds began to disappear recently from parts of northeastern Europe, whole regions cooperated in campaigns to induce the birds to return. Pollution controls were instituted, telephone lines raised or lowered so that they would no longer interfere with the birds' flight patterns and new buildings provided with store-attracting chimneys. The stork population has begun to rise again, and so have the hopes of their delighted hosts.

Swallows are often thought to be sacred, or at least lucky, because they are usually the first birds to return each spring. Swallows are generally good-luck birds but it is unlucky to kill one. If a swallow builds a nest above one's window they may expect to be taking a trip. A nest under the eaves of a house brings good luck to its inhabitants but if it abandons its nest on a house this is a sign of the burning down of the house.

The whippoorwill, because of its dark color and its nocturnal habits, has long been associated with the occult. Moreover, it is often heard just before dawn, when evil spirits are considered particularly powerful. The spirits are presumably getting in their last licks before they must disappear with the crowing of the cock. In spring, a young woman who hears the first call of the whippoorwill should listen carefully. One call means the man of her dreams will turn up. Two calls mean she will have to wait another year.

Some American Indians used to say that if you hear two whippoorwills singing together ("hoin hoin"), you should shout, "no!" If the birds cease at once, the hearer can expect to die shortly. If you hear a whippoorwill near your house, it may be carrying a message of impending death. Even if you cannot see the bird, point your finger in the direction of the sound and "shoot it." That will counter the evil.

Be especially careful not to destroy whippoorwill eggs. For each one you destroy, it is said, a member of your family will suffer misfortune. It is not quite as bad if you kill a wren or destroy its nest, you will only break a bone during the coming year. It's a good idea to never disturb the nest of any birds or bad luck will follow.

The stories of wolves as foster parents seem to be almost irresistible to many people, and they have cropped up from time to time since antiquity. According to ancient legend, Romulus and Remus who were suckled by a she-wolf were the founders of Rome.

For many centuries, Romans thought of themselves as Sons of the Wolf, and in other countries legends persist of human children reared by wolves. Such a "wolf-boy" was picked up in Lucknow, India, in 1954, and there have been others but evidence to prove is often vague, unreliable, and based on assumptions without proof. No case has ever been authenticated by scientific observers, and there have been no such reports for a long time.

If you see a wolf yawning, it is a warning to beware of empty promises. The ancients believed it was bad luck just to catch sight of a wolf and that, if he saw you before you saw him, you would lose your voice. If you spoke of a wolf, one would appear-probably with hostile intent. He would not attack a flock of sheep, however, if the shepherd kept a careful count of them.

There are also a great number of myths about animals. Animals have been included from early times in these thoughts. Some border on the ridiculous and make one wonder how they ever got started. Call them misconceptions, delusions, beliefs, falsehoods, or fantasy but don't take the list below too seriously, as the above definition implies. While there may be some justification for the introspections there is no scientific basis for the assertions.

Bees do not collect honey; they collect nectar, which is changed to honey within the bee's body. A robin hunting on the lawn and cocking his head as though he were listening is merely trying to bring his eye into position so that he can see where the worm is. Bird's eyes (with few exceptions) are set in the sides of their heads, and they see out to the sides rather than straight ahead; they do not have bifocal vision as humans.

Camel's hair brushes are never made of camel's hair, but usually from the tails of squirrels. Fine fabrics are woven from the fleece of the two-humped or Bactrian camel. The camels are not shorn but obligingly drop their hair in clumps, which are retrieved by the caretakers. The hair of the one-humped Arabian camel, or dromedary, is not used for fabrics as it is too short.

The same is true for catgut; it is not made from the intestines of cats, and never has been. Catgut comes from the intestines of sheep. That animals have eyes that can actually glow in the sense that a firefly can glow-that is, eyes that create other than reflect light is equally false. There has to be some light, at least, to be reflected; if not, neither a cat's eyes, nor any other creature's will be visible.

If those who selected the dove as a symbol of peace knew what Konrad Z. Lorenz knows about them, they might have made a different choice. Lorenz, an expert on animal behavior, put a male turtledove and a female ringdove in a cage together and left for Vienna. On his return he was horrified to find the turtledove prostrate on the floor of the cage, his featherless back a dripping bloody mass. The female "harbinger of peace" was methodically pecking away at what was left of her mate's back.

Among the rather mean little myths so often inflicted upon children is that dragonflies may sew your eyelids together. As a matter of fact, dragon flies don't even have stingers and are quite harmless, except to the mosquitoes and gnats they catch and consume on the wing. Similarly, fish as brain food doesn't hold water. The myth arose from the fact that the nerve tissue which forms a part of the brain is rich in phosphorus, and fish do provide phosphorus-containing compounds. But so do meat, poultry, eggs, and milk.

That hippo s sweat blood-is false. The hippopotamus exudes an oily reddish fluid from various large pores in its thick skin apparently the fluid is a kind of skin-conditioner which the hippopotamus needs to prevent dried and cracking skin when out of the water. That this secretion becomes both more copious and redder than usual. It does look very much like blood but is not.

Much like the belief that oysters are safe to eat only during the months that incorporate the letter "r", the pig's reputation for getting dirty is ill-deserved. Even in fairly close confinement a pig will select a place in which to defecate and repeatedly use that spot and that spot only. Most domestic animals are indiscriminate in this respect.

In America the pig early received the reputation of "liking" filth, because in New England it was usually kept in the worst place on the farm-in a dark sty under the barn. In their natural state, pigs are forest-roaming creatures. When the day is hot, pigs will wallow in the mud-but not because they like dirt. Pigs have no perspiration apparatus and this is their way of lowering the temperature of the skin.

Pigs are also at times maligned for eating garbage. In captivity, of course, they eat what they are fed. It is well to recall that of all domestic animals their preferred diet is closest to that of human beings. Finally, it is often said that pigs cannot swim, because if they try they will cut their own throats with their fore hooves. This, also, is nonsense. They can swim perfectly well.

That salmon die after spawning is true of only the United States Pacific Coast variety. It does not apply to the other 9 or so salmon species.

Few creatures excite such a mixture of awe, fear, and fascination as snakes, few are the subject of so many myths and folk beliefs. One of the oldest is that it was a "snake" in the Garden of Eden which was responsible, in John Milton's words, for bringing "death into the world." But there is no reference to a snake in Genesis; it is, rather, a "serpent" that tempted Eve. Serpents, in antiquity, were not necessarily snakes; any creeping thing, especially if venomous or noxious, was called a serpent. In the fifteen and sixteenth centuries, the term was applied to a variety of creatures, including both salamanders and crocodiles. Admittedly the temptation of Eve by a crocodile does seem to verge on the ridiculous.

Snakes do not swallow their young to protect them. Big snakes sometimes eat little snakes. The digestive juices of snakes are so quick-acting and strong they can in a short time turn bone into powder that any young swallowed are consumed, not protected.

Snakes don't have poisonous stingers in the ends of their tails. Some, like the red-bellied mud snake have sharp, spiny scales there; and if handled, the mud snake will strike with its tail. The scale is however only about one sixteenth of an inch long and is not poisonous. Quite obviously, another myth sometimes expressed-that snakes have been known to kill trees by striking them with the poisonous tips of their tails-cannot be true. Nor can any snake kill a full-grown tree either by striking it or biting it.

That Saint Patrick drove the snakes out of Ireland is doubtless regarded by most people as a charming old tale not to be taken seriously. But it might be pointed out that many islands do not have and, so far as can be determined, never have had snakes. Nor do many take seriously the mythical glass snake, which upon being dismembered can reassemble itself; or the hoop snake, which is not mythical but certainly does not roll away, its tail in its mouth (it is said sometimes to roll after its victim), in which case the victim is supposed to run uphill).

The coach whip snake can't whip its tormentors or enemies; it just looks like a coach whip, and is entirely harmless. There is actually a legless lizard, not a snake (lizards have eyelids and ear openings, snakes do not), which will grow a new tail, as many lizards can, if the original tail is broken off. But it cannot reunite its original tail with its body.

Unlike the nonexistent glass snake, the milk snake, like the coach whip, actually exists; but it does not milk cows. Even the most patient bovine is scarcely going to stand still for double rows of needle-sharp teeth. Actually, milk snakes are a great help to the farmer, for they feed upon the mice that feed upon the feed.

The puff adder (puffing adder, hissing adder, or hog nose, by all of which names and others the small American snake is known) is perfectly harmless. Contrary to what many think, it does not blow poisonous vapor at its foes nor can it inflict a wound; even if it could, the wound would not be envenomed, since the puff adder hasn't any venom sacs. All it does is try-most successfully-to look and sound very fearsome when aroused.

Some think that snakes cannot regurgitate their food because their teeth point toward the rear. This is nonsense. Snake teeth are generally very short; and snakes, especially if they are handled shortly after having eaten, can and often do regurgitate whole, large animals like squirrels and rabbits.

That the pilot black snake, Elaphe, leads copperheads and rattlesnakes back to their dens in time of danger is one of those myths reflecting the human tendency to see the world of humankind reflected in the world of other kind. The fact is that the pilot snake is simply more active than his lethal companions, with whom he often shares a den during the winter. In early spring, when the snakes come out of the den to sun during midday before actually leaving it, any sign of danger sends them scurrying back. The pilot snake just scurries faster; he isn't "leading' the others back, he's simply getting there first.

That snakes both charm and can be charmed also belongs in the folk myth category. Birds know snakes to be enemies; but sometimes they will try to decoy a snake away from the nest by approaching the snake closely. If the bid miscalculates the snake's striking distance, it will suffer the consequences not of having been "charmed," but of having been a poor judge of distance. Snakes do not, in fact, have ears; they sense vibrations in the earth rather than hear sounds as people do.

Cobras are not "charmed" by flutes. They sway in time with the flute because it is trying to get into position to strike. It is up to the charmer to keep the flute in motion so that the cobra cannot do so. He too had better be a good judge of distance or suffer the consequences.

There's no truth in the old folk belief that if you cut off the head of a snake, it won't die until sunset. No doubt the belief arose because the reflex system of snakes continues to operate after death. In fact, in the higher animals this may also happen; all the organs do not "die" at once. But in snakes the tendency is more pronounced; a snake's heart may continue to beat, for example for many hours after decapitation. It may even go right on beating after sunset, depending on when the snake was beheaded. But a headless snake is scarcely "alive."

Those cowboys or campers who encircle their sleeping bags with rope in the belief that snakes won't cross it are relying on a dangerous myth. Snakes don't at all mind crawling over ropes, as repeated experiments have proved.

As is true of flying fish, no snakes can actually fly, though some people believe they can. There is a species found in southeastern Asia and other locations that can glide for short distances by extending a webbed membrane running along each side of its body. But it cannot ascend, only descend by gliding.

A tale often told and often believed is the, "Fang in the Boot." Someone is bitten by a poisonous snake and dies. Years later, the man's son puts on the father's boot and, scratched by the still-embedded fang, dies. Occasionally the tale even involves the third generation: a grandson puts on the boot and is killed also. A large rattlesnake's fangs might be able to pierce a pair of thin leather boots and kill the first man, but that would be the end of it. Even if it did, it would lose its potency with time and exposure.

Finally, venomous snakes do not reserve their poison for their enemies, as is sometimes thought. They use it for a most practical reason: to kill their prey. They are themselves immune to their own venom if they swallow it.

Lastly, we leave the tales of snakes to deal with the myths of wolves, they are not as reported in some reports the most ferocious of creatures, wicked enemies of men who continually band together in huge hunting packs, sometimes numbering hundreds, and kill and eat human beings.

Recent scientific studies have demonstrated that the wolf is not particularly ferocious. Basically, he is friendly and more sensitive than the dog, with a complicated and subtle social organization. Wolves do not customarily hunt in large packs; their howling is not a hunting cry and does not frighten other animals. Like all animals they get their food the easiest way they can, and with the least risk. Thus, much of their prey is mice, squirrels, and rabbits; but also, unfortunately from man's point of view, lambs and calves are also targets. It is chiefly in winter that wolves form packs to hunt larger game. The pack is of moderate size-very often only a family group consisting of an old couple and their mature offspring.

Stories of wanton attacks by wolves on human beings are nonsense. There is not a single verified case in North America of a wolf attacking a human, much less eating one. Eulogists agree that if a wolf ever attacked a person it would have to be one infected by rabies, not uncommon among wolves, foxes etc.

We end with a whirlwind review of traits attributed to our animal friends that are suspect: The claims are stated and then taken to task in verse.

Bats are drawn to human hair and will become tangled therein/blind as a bat.

Don't believe what is said
Bats won't get in your head
Also untrue about their sight
They see well except at night

Bears often hug their human victims to death.

This report with much delight
Another myth that isn't right
That wouldn't be very polite
Or something you would invite

A bee dies after stinging a human.

My demise after a single sting
May have a familiar ring
But when all said and done
Be prepared for more than one

Birds only sing at sunset and dawn.

Contrary to common belief
Our chords get relief
The song of the bird
Can always be heard

Bulls are infuriated by the color red.

The reason for their discontent
Actually comes from movement
It is untrue what is said
Bulls are not infuriated by red

Camels store water in their humps.

The origin of the camel's tank
Is not from the water they drank
But no argument in the desert land
They are the best for crossing sand

Cats are smarter than dogs, but dogs have getter personalities.

The fact is difficult to depart
That cats and dogs are both smart
Because dogs are man's best friend
A better personality they pretend

Centipedes have one hundred legs.

Final analysis of the balance sheet
Says centipedes don't have a hundred feet
Whatever the count it doesn't encumber
Wonder if they worry about the number

It doesn't hurt a cow when it's branded.

The method on which to rely
The mark is to identify
Cattle avoid receiving a brand
They don't think it grand

You can't teach old dogs new tricks. Barking dogs don't bite

Watch what dogs do with sticks
Yes, they can learn new tricks
It is said barking dogs don't bite
But reality says they might

Dogs sense the death of its master even though they are separated by many miles.

A dog can't sense the last breath
Of his masters impending death
Whether close by or far apart
They are just not that smart

Goats eat shoes and tin cans.

Goats have a varied diet
Watching them eat is a riot
Cans and shoes don't qualify
I can not tell you a lie

It does not bother or pain a lobster to be cooked alive.

Into the pot he takes his dive
Knowing full well he won't survive
The lobster lobby should start a drive
To prevent them from being cooked alive

Mice prefer cheese to all other foods.

Although it doesn't displease
Mice don't only crave cheese
It is easy to identify
Other treats that qualify

Large octopuses can and do strangle humans.

Despite their number of arms
Octopus don't do fatal harm
Not interested in you as a meal
The reputation is a bad deal

Ostriches hide their heads in the sand.

Herd About Town

What appears to be in sand
Is only a sleight of hand
With the head used as a seat
It's just the way they eat

Owls can see in total darkness.

Great vision their eyes allow
Few see better than the owl
Whether they see in total dark
Remains a big question mark

Pigeons have a natural affinity for statues.

The tale on pigeon dung
Is a little far flung
Although it's hard to argue
They are fond of a statue

Porcupines shoot their quills when aroused.

Porcupines' protection is the quill
But he can't shoot it at will
For this fact we are glad
Especially when he is mad

The proper way to pick up a rabbit is by its ears.

Things are not as they appear
Never pick up a rabbit by an ear
You may say what the heck
But the rabbit prefers the neck

Snakes paralyze their intended victims with a hypnotic stare.

The word is out be aware

Of any snake with a stare.
But that they kill by hypnotic
Has been proven to be idiotic

Whales spout water.

What is all the rigmarole?
What comes from the blow hole?
While it may not seem debonair
All the whale blows is air

Animal Symbolism

The term "coat of arms" stems from the times when knights in battle wore protective armor from head to foot, making it impossible for them to be recognized by friend or foe. The knights solved this problem by wearing a light clothe "coat" over their armor, which was decorated with an identifying personal sign.

Since eventually a coat of arms became an important status symbol, practically every important family, town and even institutions adopted one. To avoid total confusion, a common design language had to be established if the designs were to have meaning to anyone other than the owners.

For this reason, the science of heraldry was devised. A "heraldic college" was established; a type of committee appointed by the king. The college set rules and standards for who could have a coat of arms, what materials they were made of, how the shield was to be divided, and what the crest symbolized. The college defined the meaning of each animal, plant or abstract design, the modifications required as the coat of arms was passed on from one generation to the next, the means by which special achievements and honors were to be represented and so on. This resulted in more than eight hundred special heraldic terms that describe the meaning of these symbols in the English language alone.

The first widely used symbol was devised some 3400 years ago by the Egyptian Pharaoh Ikhnaton. It took the form of a radiant sunburst to communicate the concept of a single God reigning over all creation. Since then the language of symbols has been widely used to signify more rapidly than words a vast variety of directions, cautions, concepts and objects have been developed. The decoration of a monument or a marker may be a sacred or secular symbol; it may be a civic social, professional, or a military emblem, a pictorial delineation, or some graphic record of an event or career.

Symbols represent emotions, instincts, or types of experiences-generally what the individual thinks. Early artists and sculptors often were attempting to get across a message to an audience that didn't read or write so they invented their own language of symbolisms

Animals got an early start participating and have stayed in the forefront of this practice with symbols. They are found in the Bible, heraldry, horoscope, mythology, paintings, religion, sculpture, theater, and the Zodiac. Many cultures through the ages have regarded specific animals as representing gods, power, the supernatural, and in the cases of Native Americans, used in names. The variety of the message from our friends in the animal kingdom is represented below.

Long before the buffalo appeared on our nickel or we had a bull and bear market animals were featured on coins, As early as Croesus', King of the Lydian's time, a horse head appeared on a coined stater. Greek coins of Xenophon, around 400 B. C. were marked with a Billy Goat and silver. Etruscan coins used the imprint of a bull. Macedonian silver coins, that circulated a century and half before Alexander The Great, show a lion attacking a bull and bronze fish were used as cash during the Han Dynasty in China.

The Romans have used a pantheon of animals on their coins from the antelope to the Centaur. At least the platypus, kangaroo, emu, lizard and opossum have been found on Australian coins.

Some of the animal participation in the economic world is hidden in our friend "Homonym." The definition or use of common words often eluded the relationship with animals and their influence on trade and money.

The Latin words for wealth and cash has found its way into our language via this route. In Rome, cattle were called *pecus*, and the word for a herd of cattle was *pecunia*. Since the Romans usually had to pay for cattle in cash, *pecunia* ultimately became the term for money in general. P*ecuniary* is derived from it, and our *fee*, which in Old English meant cattle, is cognate with *pecus*.

Indians took over the term for a herd of cattle and applied it directly to their coins. In Hindi a herd of zebra is called *rupa*; the Indian coin is the rupee

It is fitting that when the United States began to issue state quarters in 1999 animals found their way on a great number. The buffalo made the cut on several but others are noted. A group of galloping mustangs appear on the 2006 Nevada coin and a horse represents Kentucky on their 2001 quarter and the 1999 Delaware coin. Wyoming went a step further using a bucking bronco on their 2007 coin.

Keeping the theme, when it was their turn, Louisiana used a pelican, Carolina a wren. It was a mallard duck for Arkansas, a Minnesota loon, and the scissor-tailed flycatcher for Oklahoma. South Dakota's ring-necked pheasant flies over Mount Rushmore and a close up of the peregrine falcon represents Idaho. California uses a condor soaring above Yosemite Valley. Wisconsin, the dairy state, shows a cow with an ear of corn and wheel of cheese. Not to be outdone, Alaska shows a brown bear, holding its fresh salmon meal and a leaping king salmon is found on the Washington state quarter.

Those interested in horoscope run into animals as representatives or symbols of more than half of the months. Aires uses the ram, Taurus the bull and Cancer the crab. The lion is the symbol for Leo, the scorpion is used for Scorpio, the goat for Capricorn and fishes represent Pisces. The Chinese Zodiac goes even further choosing an animal for each month in the year. The animal signs used are the rat, ox, tiger, rabbit, dragon, snake, horse, sheep, monkey, rooster, dog and pig.

Some unusual animals emerged as mascots during the Civil War. Ducks, bears, dogs, donkeys, raccoon and badger accompanied the troops.

The heraldry of our nation shows a real affection for the animal kingdom. The eagle is found on the flags of Iowa, Illinois, Michigan, New York, North Dakota, and Utah. Michigan adds an elk and a moose, and Utah has a beehive. Buffalo emerge on Wyoming's pennant and are joined by eagle feathers on Oklahoma's standard bearer. California uses a bear, Missouri has two. Horses prance on Pennsylvania's flag and pull a plow on South Dakota's. Louisiana features a pelican and the badger is highlighted by Wisconsin.

In addition to the eagle being a national symbol, animal's importance is acknowledged by the individual states. All have a favorite animal and bird; many have gone beyond that stage to name their representative amphibian, insect, reptile and fish. It is hard to imagine the number of designations named that run from the appaloosa horse of Idaho to the humpback whale of Hawaii.

The turkey almost made it as our national symbol. That's what Benjamin Franklin wanted. When others suggested an eagle because eagles have traditionally been symbols of power, Franklin objected. He said they had "bad moral character" because they stole food from weaker birds. On the other hand, he said, the turkey is in comparison a much more respectable bird, a true original native of America." Congress did eventually choose the eagle, but it chose the bald eagle, which is found only in North America

Lions, tigers and bears, oh my. When it comes to sports few animals have been overlooked as mascots and nicknames. College teams use alligators to yellow jackets to intimidate the opposition. Birds, fish, fowl and amphibians also make the rosters. Unlike the players, most of these symbols find their way into the professional ranks whether it be baseball, football, hockey or rugby. Some become so popular that the city the team represents becomes obscure.

The auto industry gives credence to the marketability of animals. Over 30 vehicles have carried the animal banner from barracuda to wildcat in an attempt to add clarity to the products performance and enhance sales.

A great number of animals enjoy a designated holiday to celebrate their importance. See appendix for more detailed discussion.

Animals have always had a major role as symbols. Few have been overlooked in this important silent form of communication. The list below will assist your understanding.

aardvark, a tendency to hide from problems
ant, patience, strength, stamina
anteater frugality, prevision
ape uncleanness, malice, cunning, sin
ass, stupidity, humility, patience, pacer
badger supernatural, mischief, playfulness
bantam cock, pluckiness, priggishness
bat, blindness
bear, ill temper, uncouthness, strength, fortitude, resurrection
beaver, industriousness, vigilance, peacefulness
bee, industry, immorality, purity, order, rebirth
beehive, virtues, education, faith, abundance in the Promised Land, piety
beetle, blindness
birds, transcendence, the soul, a spirit
bird flying, rebirth
boar, ambivalent intrepidity, lust, gluttony
buffalo, supernatural power, strength, fortitude
bull, strength, straight forwardness, masculine, royalty
bull-dog, pertinacity
butterfly, sportiveness, living in pleasure, resurrection
caterpillar, life, metamorphosis.
calf, lumpish ness, cowardice
camel, humility, willingness, obstinacy
caribou, travel, mobility
cat, deceit, stealth, desire, liberty, lust, laziness
cicada, demon of light and darkness, poetry

conch, vigilance, overbearing insolence, wisdom
cougar, leadership, courage, power, swiftness, balance
cow, the Great Mother, productive power, plenty, procreative
crow, longevity
coyote, the trickster, humor, charm, prankster
crocodile, hypocrisy, devourer, guardian of the door
cuckoo, cuckoldom
deer, swiftness, medication, meekness
dog, hypocrisy, fidelity. watchfulness, nobility
dolphin, sea power, safety, swiftness
donkey, patience, stupidity, obstinacy
dog, vendibility, dirty habits
dove innocence, harmlessness, life, spirit, soul, gentleness, peace, purity
duck, deceit, French, canard, a hoax; chatter, deceit
eagle, majesty, inspiration, solar, victory, pride, authority, courage, military
eel, phallic, slipperiness
elephant, sagacity, ponderosity, strength, fidelity, patience, wisdom
elk, supernatural power
ermine, chastity purity, innocence
falcon, solar, aspiration, victory, freedom
fish, phallic, fecundity, procreation power of the waters, faith, life
fly, feebleness, insignificance, evil, corruption
fox, cunning, artifice, slyness, cunning, hypocrisy, craftiness
frog and toad, inspiration, lunar, fertility, fecundity, eroticism, sin
goat, lasciviousness, masculinity, vitality, creative energy
goose, conceit, folly, solar, breath, the wind
gull, gullibility
grasshopper, old age, wisdom, nobility
hare, timidity, rebirth, rejuvenation resurrection, intuition
hawk, rapacity, penetration, power, royalty, nobility
hedgehog, evil, rejuvenation
hen, maternal care, procreation, providence, maternal care
hippopotamus, bounty and protection
horse, speed, grace, intellect, mind, reason, wisdom, nobility, strength, wisdom
horse shoe, good luck, protection against evil
hyena, vice, impurity, instability, inconstancy, two-faced
ibis, perseverance, truth, justice

jackdaw, brain assumption, empty conceit
jaguar, power of darkness
jay, senseless chatter
kingfisher, calm, beauty, dignity, speed
kitten, playfulness
lamb, innocence, sacrifice, gentleness, meekness, purity, resurrection
lark, cheerfulness
leopard, cruelty, ferocity, aggression, intrepidity
lion, noble courage, majesty, strength, courage, fortitude, justice, law, military might, king of the beasts
lizard, silence, wisdom good fortune
lobster, longevity
lynx, suspicious vigilance, keenness of eye sight
magpie, garrulity, good fortune
mole, blindness, obtuseness, power of darkness
monkey, tricks
moose, headstrong
mouse, incessant movement, senseless agitation
mountain lion, liberty, vigilance, courage
mule, obstinacy
nightingale, forlornness
octopus, thunder, depicting lunar phrases
ostrich, stupidity, truth justice and law
owl, wisdom, darkness, death
ox, patience, strength, solar fertility
oyster, the womb, birth and rebirth, initiation
panther, boldness, cunning, swiftness, strength,
parrot, mocking verbosity, imitation, unintelligible, repetition
partridge, fertility, fecundity
peacock, pride, immorality, longevity, love,
pelican, sacrifice, charity, piety
pheasant, divine royalty, nobility, uniqueness, good fortune
pigeon, cowardice
praying mantis, prayer, adoration
quail, good luck spring
pig, obstinacy, dirtiness
puppy, empty-headed, conceit

rabbit, fecundity
ram, virility, creative, energy, procreative powers
rat, death, decay the underworld, quick-witted
raven, ill luck, prophecy, darkness of evil, destruction of war
rhinoceros, ferocity, protection
salamander, connects water and earth
scallop shell, birth, baptism, resurrection, life everlasting, pilgrimage of life.
scarab, resurrection, transcendence.
scorpion, destructive force, disaster darkness
sea horse, confidence, grace, authority, power, possession individuality, secrecy
serpent, wisdom
sheep, silliness, timidity, helplessness
snail, slowness, voluptuousness, sin, laziness
snake, encircled everlasting life in heaven.
spider, wildness, weaver of destiny, protection from harm
spider web, human frailty
squirrel, avarice greed
stag, cuckoldom, renewal creation fire the dawn
stallion, fire power
stork, creation, coming of spring new life
swallow, a sunshine friend, hope coming of spring, good fortune, motherhood
swan, grace, bird of life, dawn of day
swine, filthiness, greed, fertility, prosperity, gluttony, lust, anger, unbridled passion
tiger, ferocity, royalty cruelty strength
tortoise, chastity, the waters, the moon, the earth mother, immortality, fecundity, regeneration
turkey, cock, official insolence, thunder rain
turtle, longevity slowness, love, conjugal fidelity
unicorn, spirit of purity, innocence, childhood
vulture, rapine, protection shelter destruction voracity
weasel, purity, chastity
whale, power of the water, regeneration, death, rebirth
whopping crane, freedom
woodpecker, persistence, magic guardian of kings and trees
wolf, cruelty, savage ferocity, the earth evil the devouring fierceness
wolverine, revenge, understanding aggression, protection against attackers,

multilevel protection, standing your ground, fierceness
woodpecker, prophecy, magic, power worm, cringing, death dissolution the earth

After reviewing the above symbolisms it is not surprising to find a great number of animal representations in our nation's capital. Although the elephant and donkey get most of the ink as representatives of the Republican and Democratic parties, not surprisingly horses, lions, and eagles also appear in abundance. Other animals are used in a variety of scenarios. They are found on statues, paintings, doorways, frieze, pediments, and bridges. Without considering the statues at the zoo, here are some examples.

The Department of Agriculture Building on Independence Avenue displays heads of 76 turkeys, 30 eagles, 183 horses, 132 bulls, and 152 rams. American Wildlife building follows with 174 wildlife figures depicted and grouped by their ecological region in the United States. The Department of Labor features ram, cows, lions, snakes, eagles, dolphins, and triton.

Over 40 grotesques of all types of animals appear on the Washington National Cathedral. The list includes grasshoppers, praying mantis, rhinoceros, ram, iguana, rattlesnakes and snails. Ducks, parrots, and owls represent birds and domestic animals are represented by cats, dogs, and hamsters. Penguin, lobster, giraffe, eagles, elephants and pigs are also included.

Embassies throughout the city display a variety of unusual animal presentations mostly showcasing animals of their region.

It's good to see Washington take the lead in animal recognition even if they were late comers to paying their respect.

Loosely aliened with superstitions, myths and symbols is heuristics. Making decisions is not always easy. When more than one solution is available we often fall back to heuristics from the Greek word, "discover." Our discoveries also come from experience setting the stage for our choice. If there is no familiarity rules of thumb come into play. We learn from others how to proceed in a pre-selected route.

Animals have also played a role in this topic. You may find some of the rules below useful in areas you have not yet explored. A caution, as with the other categories, is appropriate for the validity of these guides.

1. When cars look as big as ants, it's time to open the parachute.
2. A bear can outrun, out climb, and out swim a human.

3. When fleeing a bear, remember your only chance is to run downhill.
4. One skilled person can manage five hundred bee colonies.
5. A skilled beekeeper can get as much as 100 pounds of honey per hive per year.
6. Study the bird, not the field guide. The bird will fly away. The guide won't.
7. The single best clue to a bird's identity is the shape of its bill.
8. You need at least 1 bull for every 15 cows.
9. Don't choose a camel that trembles while sitting.
10. If you don't want a cat to jump in your lap, don't make eye contact with it.
11 If you paint the inside of your chicken coop orange, your chickens will lay more eggs.
12. The averages cow belches twice a minute, producing ten gallons of methane a day.
13. A quart jar will hold 1,000 crickets.
14. Zigzag to outrun a crocodile.
15. Half of the deer hit by cars are struck in May or November.
16. A kennel should be two times the length of the dog that will occupy it.
17. The African elephant has an ear shaped like Africa; the Indian elephant has an ear shaped like India.
18. To find an elephant, look within 300 meters of water.
19. Your fishing pole should be twice the length of your arm.
20. The further north, the smaller Canada geese; the farther west, the darker the color.
21. Plan on using one pack horse for every 150 pounds you need to carry.
22. Rub a horse's face and ears as gently as you would pet a cat.
23. Plan on losing about 33 percent of your lobster pots each year to storms and heavy seas.
24. One ostrich egg will serve 24 people for brunch.
25. If a polar bear charges you, dodge to the right, Eskimos say most polar bears are left-pawed.
26. It takes the profit from four pigs to pay the cost of keeping a sow.
27. For capturing pythons, anacondas, boas and other large constrictors, it is wise to have one person for every 4 or 5-feet of snake.
28. A rat can pass through a hole half the size of a quarter.
29. Plan on 11 reindeer for every 75 pounds of supplies.
30. You can make one sweater for every two pounds of wool you shear from a sheep.

Robert C. Layton

Group Names

When we gather in groups we are known by many names. At home we are a family, in school we are either teachers or students, at church we are a congregation, at a movie or performance an audience, at a sporting event we could be a team or spectators. At the mall we are designated shoppers, at a restaurant we are customers or diners. Sometimes it's our occupation that defines us, whether doctors, lawyers, plumbers, salesmen or actors.

Animals are identified by a much broader range of designations. Birds and animals of all kinds have always played an important part in mankind's survival. Man hunted and trapped them for his food, and made use of their skins and feathers for his clothing. As time passed he began to appreciate the different species and to take notice of their various habits and skills.

For every collection of beasts of the forest and for every gathering of birds of the air there became a private name so that none is confused with the other. Some very unusual descriptions developed for these assembled creatures.

Most everyone is familiar with a gaggle of geese, a pack of wolves, and a herd of elephants. Terms such as crash, murder and destruction, as they pertain to animal throngs, are not as well-known. These are in fact, used to identify groups of rhinoceros, crows, and wildcats.

There are a great number of these peculiar classifications. All are informative, some humorous, while others seem to border on the ridiculous. The etymology of this subject is an interesting examination of terms of venery, collective nouns, and labels of assemblage. The study gives credence to the development out of necessity and suggests the probable emergence from one of the following sources.

1. Onomatopoeia: i.e. a murmuration of starlings, a peep of chickens, a tittering of magpies.
2. Characteristics: for example a leap of leopards, a skulk of fox and a labor of

moles. This approach is by far the largest family.

3. Appearance: includes a knot of toads, a bouquet of pheasants, and a cloud of flies.
4. Habitat: for instance, a kennel of dogs, a nest of rabbits and a rookery of albatross.
5. Comment pro or con: reflecting the observer's point of view; illustrations include a richness of martens, cowardice of curs and an obstinacy of buffalo.
6. Error: resulting from an incorrect transcription by a scribe or printer faithfully preserved in the corrupted form by subsequent compilers; probably the most descriptive in this category is a school of fish, originally "shoal, for their habitat."

Some of the following group identifications appear at first glance to be inappropriate; certainly not commonly used. Accompanying lexical support, attesting to the suitability, removes some of the mystery.

Asses, Coffle- to fasten together, number of persons, band, company, group, especially a caravan

Bees, Swarm- a crowd, horde, multitude, throng, community

Caterpillars, Army- a great number, a vast multitude

Cats, Harem- a place where a Moslem keeps his wives/concubines
clowder- a group of cats

Cows, Kine- double plural of cow, cattle

Cranes, Meiny- a crowd, throng, multitude

Ducks, Fleet- most generally reserved for groups of ships, trucks, buses, air planes etc. acting together under one control

Eagles, Convocation- a calling together; an assemblage by summons- generally ecclesiastical/academia-a meeting, a council

Eels, Wisp- small bunch/bundle usually hay or sticks, flock

Fish, Fere,- a companion, a mate, together

Grouse, Jug- to come together

Hares, Peltry- bearing skins collectively

Hawks, Cast- replica, copy, breeding, multiplication

Horses, Coffle- a caravan, to fasten together
Ruck- heap or stack large number or quantity, multitude

Hounds, Suit- a group of things forming a set or series

Lions, Troop- band, company, corps, outfit

Martins, Richness- the interesting quality of something that has a lot of different features or aspects ▸

Oyster, Park- common, collective, communal, stew- a pool, tank or a small pond fish live in

Peacocks, Muster- collect, gather, summon, assemble, marshall,

Salmon, Draft- the amount of fish taken in one drawing of the net amount taken in one breath, liquid at one drink, drawing of beer, money, or air-taking for military service

Storks, Phalanx- collect, gather, shore-up, assemble, round-up

Swallows, Rush- a sudden movement forward, especially by a crowd of people

Tortoise, Bale- package, packet, accumulation, bunch

A more detailed explanation of other unusual collective nouns for gathering of animal throngs is discussed below with emphasis on how the designation came about..

A cete of badgers- The best guess is that it may be the old Chaucerian word for "city"

A singular of boars- At first thought it seems strange to use singular as a designate for a group of anything. Singular is obviously an English scribe's transliteration of sanglier, the French word for "boar" which was, in its turn, a French transliteration of "boar" in Latin, singularis-porcus. Now, singularis porcus certainly seems to imply that the boar travels alone, hence needs, and deserves no group term-until one recalls that in Latin, as in English the word "singular" means both "solitary" and "extraordinary, whereas the exclusive sense of "solitary" or "single" was usually consigned to singulus. Singularis, sanglier and singular all mean "extraordinary"

A dule of doves is a corruption of the French deuil; mourning. The soft, sad uttering of the dove has always evoked an association with mourning.

A trip of goats- A widely used term it could come from the Icelandic thrypa, meaning "flock" or it could be a corruption of "tribe."

A charm of goldfinch- This may be one of the best known collective terms, widely used and beautifully descriptive of the flock of birds that in autumn or winter gather round thistle heads and feeders, their gold plumage glittering in the sunlight. Investigation shows, or seems to, that charm is a corruption of cherme, chyme, or chirping and referred originally to the sound that the birds made not to their appearance.

Webster may assist to defuse that theory. Down the list of definitions under charm appears "a hypothetical property of certain heavy elementary particles, described by a quantum number, observed only in matter excited to very high energies, and postulated to be a fourth quark.

Milton is quoted "with charm of earliest birds", and Charles Kingsley wrote of "a "charm of birds."

A battery of hens- How chickens originally got the same designation as guns is a mystery. Originally used for metal objects or utensils collectively, the animal use evolved later.

A siege of herons- any continued endeavor to gain possession or to overcome the opposition is commonly referred to as a siege. The heron standing at the waterside, or in the water, motionless for hours, waiting for an unwary fish to pass by, certainly qualifies as an exemplary for use of this name.

A kindle of kittens- Kin, kindred, and the German Kinder are related to this word from the Middle English kinklen. To kindle literally means "to give birth."

A covey of partridges- Here is an interesting etymological journey: the Latin cubare means "to be lying down" (both concubine, to be lying down with, and incubate, to be lying down on, also derived from this root). It becomes covee in Old French, whence cove or covy in Middle English. Thus it refers to nesting habits.

A sounder of swine- This is one of those words that suffered some interesting sea-changes hopping back and forth across the English Channel. Originally it was the Old English word sunor, meaning herd. The Norman French adopted it and it became Gallicized to soundre. Since Norman French was the language of all the earliest hunting treatises, and thus the principal source of hunting terms, the word returned to England as sounder, with the English none the wiser that they were borrowing back their own term.

A pod of seals- The derivation of this word is obvious, since a pod contains several peas. It was borrowed by sailors to describe groups of seals.

A rafter of turkeys- Probably not what you think, if you see birds sitting on a beam. The term is related to raft in the sense of "a large and often motley collection of people and things, as a raft of books," according to Webster. It is also related to raff, which means a collection of things, and appears in some interesting variations in “riffraff” and “raffish.

A bale of turtles- Probably one of the erroneous terms, a corruption of dule, since early scribes sometimes confused turtle doves with turtles.

A gam of whales- To gam is to gossip. A whaling voyage could last as long as three years, so when two whalers encountered each other on some remote sea, it called for a gam, an exchange of crews via whaleboats and the "gamming chair." It was a happy time for whale men and, obviously, the whales' habit of sporting playfully on the surface of the sea gave rise to this fanciful term.

A fall of woodcocks. The Old English Dictionary explains this term as an alleged name for a covey or flight of woodcock. An early writing included this, "Consider their coming, which is so sudden (as to divers of the kinds) that it is as if they dropped down upon us from above. In woodcocks especially it is remarkable that upon a change of the wind to the east.

Below we find the entomology of other group designations that are used for several animals. The inspection of these general classifications gives additional clarification to the origin of animal gatherings.

Brood refers to the young of certain animals, such as birds or fish; especially, a group of such animals hatched at one time and cared for by the same mother. Brood goes back to Old English brod ("offspring, brood"), which can be traced back to a Germanic root meaning "a warming, hatching, rearing of young," which in turn is based on an Indo-European root meaning "to boil." Brood is also used for the young of bees before they issue from the brood cells and for the pupae of ants.

It is easy to understand the term "drove" comes from cattle being driven, perhaps from the farm to the market or from the market to the slaughterhouse. The word goes back to Old English draft ("drove"), a derivative of the verb drifan ("to drive"), which is based on an Indo-European root meaning "to drive or push."

According to the Old English Dictionary, the animal sense of drove was established before the word was extended to apply to a crowd of humans, especially when moving in concert.

Flock defines a group of animals, especially birds or goats or sheep, that live, travel, or feed together. Flock goes back to Old English flocc ("band of people" perhaps related to folc, "folk"). Today the use of flock for a group of people, especially one under the leadership of a single authority, is only as a transfer from the animal sense. A large number of anything can now be called a flock.

A “herd” is a group of animals of any kind feeding or traveling together. The word goes back to Old English heord ("herd"), which is based on an Indo-European heord which has its foundation on an Indo-European root meaning "herd." Extended, herd refers, usually disparagingly, to a large company of people. The herd is the common people. Used initially as a collective term or a term of assemblage it has now expanded to encompass a keeper of animals. The application is restricted to use in combination with the animal being kept, i. e. goatherd, shepherd, or swineherd.

Pack, in addition to the familiar pack of lies, a pack of cards and a pack of cigarettes, not to mention the popular six pack, is used for a number of wild animals living together. In an early reference William of Malmesbury in his History recalls: “Edward the Confessor took the greatest delight to follow a pack of swift hounds in pursuit of game.”

The collective nouns that describe groups of birds use a wide variety of uncommon terms to describe the flyers gathered. In addition to the more common flight, flock, gaggle, bevy and brood the following terms are used.

Bitterns, cranes and herons gather in a siege, cloughs are seen in chatterings, and coots hang out in converts and rafts. Murder is the group term for crows and doves are referred to as dole or pitying, while ducks congregate in baldlings and teams. Eagles meet in convocations, falcons in a cast and finches in a troubling. Geese are in a gaggle while gathered on the ground but become a skein while together in flight. Finch are referred to as a charm or troubling and grouse are called a covey when found in groups.

Hawks gather in a leash, jays band together, larks go by exaltation and magpies use tittering or tiding to define their groups. It’s a paddling of mallards, a watch of nightingales and a parliament of owls when identifying these clustered birds. Ravens are called an unkindness and rooks a clamor in their gatherings. More unusual perhaps is the starling refereed to as a murmuration or sparrows in a quarrel; challenged by the designation of wedge for swans and knob of teal. Not to forget turkey’s found in rafts, dules, crops, or rafters.

Herd About Town

The following sentences incorporate labels our ancestors used to identify animals gathered in a group. See how many you can figure out and try some of your own. See list following matching game to check your answers.

Apes use shrewdness in their shrewdness.
You can not rent a room in a beaver lodge.
You can't ride a bee's bike.
Cats glaring, doubt and litter have multiple meanings.
Clams sleep in a water bed.
A crow's murder is not a crime.
A parcel of deer is not a package.
A balding of ducks is doesn't have anything to do with hair.
Eagles live in convocation.
Have you ever seen a deer on a leash?
Ferrets transact business in a body.
Finches attend charm school.
Do fish attend school in schools?
A frog can't tie a knot nor can anyone with a string of ponies.
A hen's battery won't start a car (or light a flashlight.)
Herons siege upon their prey with vigor.
A leap of leopards is not a jump.
Locust enjoys the plaque.
Magpies wish each other happy tidings.
Martin richness is not related to values.
A nightingale's watch can't tell time. Also true of goat's clock.
An oyster spat is not disagreeable and their bank doesn't have money.
An owl's parliament is not a body of government.
Peacocks in ostentation are often ostentatious.
A plover's congregation is not religious.
A plum of a seal doesn't grow in a tree.
A squirrel's dray does not have wheels.
You wouldn't want to watch television in a den of snakes.
Do swine hear better in a sounder?
Turkeys can be in a rafter with their feet on the ground
Do turtles bale hay?

A vulture's peal adds on.
You probably wouldn't want a wreath of worms.

Here is another chance to match your wits against those earlier pioneers of clan terminology. Help the animals in the left hand column find their appropriate group listed on the right. See answers under group matching in answer section.

1. beavers	a. bask
2. bees	b. caravan
3. camels	c. cloud
4. crocodiles	d. confusion
5. donkeys	e. down
6. ducks	f. exaltation
7. elk	g. fall
8. giraffe	h. fry
9. grasshoppers	i. gang
10. guinea fowl	j. labor
11. hares	k. paddling
12. horses	l. race
13. larks	m. society
14. moles	n. stable
15. ponies	o. string
16. termites	p. tower
17. woodcocks	q. wood

The following list will assist you with checking your answers in both sentences and matching exercise. When an animal is used more than once, the following designations assist in deciphering the correct answers.

Albatross rookery, flock
Antelope herd
Ants colony, army, state, swarm, nest
Apes apery, shrewdness
Ass pace, herd, drove

Herd About Town

Auks colony, flock
Badgers cete
Bears sleuth, sloth
Beavers lodge, society
Beesbike, cluster, fry, game, hive, nest, parlin, peck, rabble, squadron
Birds aviary, bitterly, concent, dissimulation, erge, geege, flurry, layden, leash, nide, passage, rush, sedge, volery, watch
Boar singular
Buffalo gang, obstinacy
Buzzard flight
Camels caravan, herd, string, train
Caterpillar`army
Caribou herd
Cats clowder, cluster, doubt, glaring, litter
Cattle armentose, armental, bunch, draft, drift, drive, drove, flote, stock
Chicken clutch, peep, wood
Clams bed
Coot covert
Cows cull, dairy, kine
Crane meiny, siege
Crocodile bask, cover, nest, raft
Crow murder
Deer game, herd, leash, parcel, park, rangall
Dogs bench, brace, kennel, pack, pedigree, regiment, team
Dolphin team
Donkey race
Dove dule
Duck balding, cletch, mob, paddling, plumb, safe, spurt, taradiddle
Eagle aerie, cast, shoal, convocation
Eggs clutch, laughter, mess,
Eels bed, bond, eelfare, strike, swarm
Elephant flock, herd, span, string
Elk gang
Ewe flock
Falcon cast, last
Ferret business, cast, fesnyng
Finch charm

Fish aquarium, brace, catch, draft, drove, fere, fishery, park, skull, warp, warren
Flies business, cloud, hatch, grist, skulk, whisk
Fox brace, cloud, burrow, crew, earth, skulked
Frog arm, knot, rain
Geese gaggle, meine, rank, skein, team, train
Giraffe tower
Gnats plaque
Goats clock, herd, rusk, tribe, trip
Goldfish troubling
Gorilla band
Grasshoppers cloud
Greyhound brace, stud
Grouse brace, brood, covey, drive, game, harvest, jug, pack
Guinea fowl confusion
Gull colony
Hare down, flick, peltry, tower, trace, trip, warren
Hawk aerie, brood, cast, mews, staff, tower, train
Hedgehog array, nest
Hens battery, brood, covey, mews, parcel, serglio
Heron hedge, rookery, passage, sedge, siege,
Hog drift, hoggery, passel
Hornet nest
Horses calvary, coffle, harras, levy, mob, ruck, rush, stable stand, stud, team,wedge
Hounds brace, clan, corrat, cry, field, harl, heap, kennel, mute, leash, pack, suit
Ibex herd
Jays band, party
Jelly fish flutter, smack, smutt
Kangaroo herd, mob, troop
Kitten kindle
Lamb cast, crop, fall, head, tail, trip
Lapwings deceit, desert
Larks ascension, bevy, exaltation, flight
Leopard leaped, lepe
Lice flock
Lions flock, pride, sault, saut, troop
Locust plague, swarm, cloud

Mackerel shoal
Magpies tidings, tittering
Mallard lute, pudding, sord(e), suit
Mares stud
Martins richness
Mice harvest, regiment, store
Minnows steam, shoal
Moles company, labor, movement
Monkeys cartload, levy, schemazzle, tribe, troop, wilderness
Mouse nest
Mules barren, mulada, pack, span
Mussel scalp
Nightingale watch
Otter catch, lodge
Owl parliament, store
Oyster bank, bed, hive, park, scalp, span, spat, tail, warp
Ox drove, her, span, stud, team
Partridges covey
Peacocks muster, ostentation, stew
Penguins colony, parcel, rookery, town
Pheasants bouquet, eye, nye, school, stew, warren
Pigeons flight, kit, loft, school
Plovers congregation, wing
Ponies string
Porpoise chorus, gam, herd, pod, turmoil
Prairie dog burrow, town
Ptarmigan covey
Quail bevy
Rabbits bury, colony, nest, warren
Rats colony
Ravens unkindness
Red deer game
Rhinoceros crash, stubbornness
Rooks building, clamor
Sand pipers fling
Sardines family
Seals bulk, crash, flock, harem, herd, plum, pod

Sharks shoal, school
Sheep cull, down, drove, flock, fold, hurtle, meine, mob, phalanx, trip
Skunk chine
Snails tribe, walk
Snakes bed, den, knot, pit, sheaf, tier
Snipes walk, wisp
Sparrows host, meine
Squirrels dray
Starlings mummuration, chattering
Storks mustering, phalanx
Swallows flight, gulp
Swan drift, eyrar, herd, sounder, team, wedge
Swine drift, doylt, drove, farce, sounder, swinery, trip
Teal bunch, knob, leash, string
Termites wood, nest, colony, swarm
Tigers ambush, den, wilderness
Toad knob, knot, nest
Tortoise dole, bale
Trout hover
Turkey rafter, crop
Turtle doves pitying
Turtles bale, dole, duet, turn
Vultures cast, peal
Walrus huddle, trio
Wasps nest, plague, society, vespiary
Weasels pack
Whales gam, grind, herd, mob, party, plumb, school, tribe
Wildcats destruction
Wolves herd, horde, mob, pack, route
Woodcocks fall
Woodpeckers decent
Worms bed, bob, clew, wreath
Zebra herd, zeal

Animals appearing in Group-other than alpha sections.

albatross
badger
bird
buffalo
chicken
crow cur
dog
dove
duck
mallard
eagle
elephant
falcon
fish
fly
fox
geese
goat
goldfinch
gopher
hawk
hen
heron
kitten
lark
leopard
martin
may fly
mole
nightingale
partridge
pheasant
rabbit
raven
seal

sheep
sparrow
starling
swan
swine
toad
turkey
turtle
whale cattle
wolf

The story below reflects on the diversity of names discussed above. Just over one hundred animals appear and only six are without a group designation. With those exceptions, the assembly name for each animal is found in the same or adjacent sentence to the one where the animal is mentioned. Where an animal is used more than once look for a second descriptive collective noun.

Many of the terms are obsolete today, but all played an important role in labeling at the time when hunting for game was vital to existence. Designations that may come to mind when considering animal groups and the chase at hand could include at least the following: assembly, aviary, menagerie, mess, migration, myriad, safari, throng, store, strain, mass, reservoir, lump, wealth, rush, unit, platoon, party, formation, bunch, detachment, cordon, column, mint, library, array, zoo, company, parcel, crowd, syndicate, clan, brace, horde, and many more. None of these terms are used in the story.

Dictionaries, word origin sources, encyclopedias, animal and juvenile books, almanacs, and other sources were consulted to locate the etymology.

See how many animals you can spot matching them with their respective group identity before checking the answer section. Some liberty with spelling has been taken to assist (?) you in your hunt.

Fowl Play

Buzzards and vultures soared overhead. Their flight, sailing the drafts, with earnest purpose was often a sign of foul play. As glide turned to dive it was apparent a tragedy had occurred at the local saloon. Closer scrutiny disclosed what had taken place. Several crows had been murdered! Fowl play indeed!

Cranky Crocodile, the areas best known investi-gator, was basking in the sun when he was called in on the case. He welcomed the assignment and started right away. The animal kingdom was in an uproar for only one clue had been developed. An army of caterpillars were reported to have witnessed the event, but they couldn't be located.

A meeting was called, hosted by the sparrows. Jays band together squawking the announcement, swans wedged in trumpeting their input, and starlings chattered their advice; all assisting in getting the message across the air waves. Giraffes were useful broadcast towers.

An impressive number of species responded. Pigeons left their loft, turkeys gobbled from the rafters, mice left their nests, geese gaggled, oyster spat, and a gang of elk joined in. Hares, although loaded down with offspring hopped in to contribute their share. Dogs packed into the building like a family of sardines and cats were littered throughout the meeting place. Rhinoceros crashed the assembly and Guinea fowl added to the confusion, hounding everyone with their awesome cry.

When the elephants herd of the gathering they swarmed in with the bees. A flock of ewe followed sheep-ishly, despite being plagued by the locust. The red deer family said they were game to help in any way they could. A string of ponies tied up one entrance and the fox trying to skulk in the rear tripped over the goat guards (no kidding).

Mules left their barren land to join the forces. Nightingales watched from a distance. As the word spread, others joined in to assist in the plan to bring the guilty one to justice. Something had to be done!

As the search began, a smack of jelly fish watched the decent of the woodpeckers, as they pursued the route of the wolves that were believed to be at the root of this calamity. A flight of swallows watched overhead and leopards leaped in to lend a hand.

Magpies brought tidings of good cheer and worked with the seal harem like peas in a pod. Not all was positive, the deceit of the lapwings tied the frogs in knots causing the hens to brood and the lions pride to be hurt, but the investigation went on.

A second assembly gathered at the other end of the borough. The Frogs, who were usually cooperative when someone croaked, toad a colony of ten-ants from a neigh boring knob and reported the termites agreed they wood help.

Trout hovered over the nearby stream to observe the proceedings. Ducks paddled along in a curios manner with mallards sord of leading the way. Even whales who normally avoided a mob joined in and dolphin enrolled on the team.

Mackerel stayed upon the shoal wishing to catch a ride with the otter or connect with the auk as they came by on their raft. Walrus huddled on the bank deciding whether they were suited to assist and swans were adrift. Only goldfish and snakes ignored the commotion; not troubling to get involved, they stayed in bed.

Through the kindness of the raven, who was dean of the institution, finches and fish were allowed to leave charm school to join the plover's congregation formed to design a plan to investigate. The event was sponsored by the richness of the martins. This meeting took place in the Rook Building at the Eagles Convocation Center.

With the owl's approval, the porcupine opened the meeting by raising the point of forming a parliament. Hawks signaled their agreement as they cast their vote from a near-by perch in the park. The monkey tribe sanctioned the move and it was shaped. The only opposition came from the peacocks who didn't think the plan would muster and the swine who thought there was a sounder way to approach the problem. The boars weren't satisfied with the singular position but remained silent.

The shrewdness of the apes got them elected chairman of the group. They immediately appointed Robin Swift in charge of maneuvers because she owned a very large dray jointly with a family of squirrels. This vehicle, yoke driven by the oxen, would be helpful in getting around with as many as would like to assist her/on the siege to find the killer. Lions were trooped in to head up the planning process and turtles doled out last minute instructions. The ferret clan kept a keen eye to make certain the committee stuck to business.

The coterie set out to develop their clues joining Cranky and his crowd. There was no horsing around; they raced right down to business, a stable group indeed. A goose, who was trained in crime, suggested they take a gander at the surrounding area where the crime occurred. Camels led the caravan, donkeys worked as fast as if they were in a race, and snails walked a quickened pace.

Skunks were given an assignment on the chine. Tigers and flamingos were elected to stand guard, so as to avoid an ambush. Hares traced down suspicious tracks that were soon identified as those of the offenders.

The trail led to Tunneltown where prairie dogs had tried to bury the evidence of their visitors. The posse realized they were on to something. They didn't pussyfoot around. Moles litterly took the bull by the horns and did the heavy underground labor making every movement count. The hideout was surrounded and soon the accused was apprehended.

At the trial, Kangaroos were trooped in to preside over the court. An election for Bale-iff was held between Tommy Tortoise and Harey Rabbit. It was a close race, with Tommy winning by a neck (a turtleneck), sending Harey back to his warren.

The case ended when the wolves were found guilty. The sentence was life in prison, an albatross that would rook them for the rest of their lives. Certainly not something they could crow about.

The next time you are with friends try to think of the various collective nouns that might describe your activity but don't try to compete with the animals for number of options available.

Animal's Reign on Weather Forecasting

Predicting the weather is an arduous task. Cloud formations, air pressure, humidity and unexpected storm patterns, play tricks and raise havoc with prognosis. Weather has its own disposition. Its mood swings make it almost impossible to gauge projections with accuracy. Weathermen work in an exasperating atmosphere; the job has a lot of pressure. It's reached the point where they are on cloud nine when correct.

Meteorologists try to predict future trends, studying data from satellites, balloons, computers, barometers and other temperature devises. Their equipment includes such aids as weather vanes, barographs, anemometers, thermometers, and hygrometers. Satellites and radar that are designed to provide timely reports, but it is still perplexing to try to anticipate tomorrow's conditions.

It is easy to cloud the issue of forecasting when the elements get twisted and things change with lightning speed. The deluge of information is hard to cope with. Granted precipitation amounts are hard to gage, cold snaps are met with a chilly response, and hot flashes come without warning. Tides rise and fall, fronts return back where they started and waves become blasts of air masses that are often hidden by a low ceiling and blown off course.

Just as in life, some can breeze through blustery conditions while others end up in a whirlwind of disgust, not having the foggiest idea how to cope. It takes a tough squall to ride out the storm. Only the hail and hardy survive. Gale Berg is one of those. She fights through the turbulent times. I don't wish to haze-up the issue, but learning nature's lessons, as she has, will serve you well in dew time. To ignore them can lead to bitter consequences.

Gale has a sunny disposition and knows how to weather the storm. Her system is simple. Avoid getting low and suffering depression by keeping a high activity load. Play it cool, channel your thoughts to stay in your own zone. A degree of awareness will undo stress. Keep a reservoir of projects to keep disorder at bay. Don't slip into the pitfall of speculation. You can avoid a slide into the black hole by staying in circulation and keeping current.

Gale recognizes that the hi-tech data and instrumentation produces a wide divergence of information received. Did you ever notice how many times you wake up to a weather pattern conflicting with what you expected from the previous evenings forecast? Some think the whole process is a snow job and weatherman stay in a fog. Others feel they are too precipitous and presumptive in their guessing.

Before all the sophistication, man approached weather interpretation from a different perspective. In those days he thought as much about his animals and livestock as about his crops or family. He took particular notice of the animals' habits and often attributed what he saw to the various quirks of weather.

With so many options it's a wonder why the animal system was ever replaced. Maybe we should work toward better understanding the messages our animal friends are sending and save the high cost development of more equipment. The next time the weatherman gives his forecast check out these gems to support or refute his judgment. You may be surprised at the number of animals that participate in this activity and the poetic approach several take.

Reviewing a selection of these observations gives a better understanding of how the process works. Most are very old and surprisingly often accurate. You may be skeptical and find some of determinations amusing but don't sell them short without giving them a chance.

Bats flitting about late in the evening foretell a fine spring or autumn day for the morrow. Beetles flying about late at evening also foreshadow a fine next day and if butterflies appear early they are sending the message of good weather.

When you see gossamer flying, be sure the air is drying. Conversely, there are a great many signs of bad weather. It appears the farmers went out of their way to find signs for needed rain.

When you hear the asses bray,
We shall have rain on that day.

However imbecilic it appears, when asses shake their ears it's also said to be sign of rain.

Bees will not swarm if a storm is near. If they stay at home, rain will come soon and you can bet on a severe winter ahead when large stores of honey are laid up.

When buffalo band together the storm god is herding them. The same for cattle when they cease their feeding and chase each other, there will be a change in the weather.

Cats lick their bodies and wash their faces when showers are approaching and watch for rain when chickens are unusually noisy. If they run for cover when it starts to rain, the shower will be brief; if they stay outside, it is going to rain all day.

A horde of cicadas is a sign of coming bad weather and the first frost will surely come six weeks after you hear the first cricket. A storm is coming if cows lie down, act fidgety, or head for the barn. Rain is on the way if they refuse to graze.

When a cow tries to scratch its ear,
It means a shower be very near,
When it begins to thump its rib with its tail,
Look out for thunder, lightning and hail.

Crows giving forth a peculiar and unusual cry herald the coming of rain. Also true when dogs become sleepy and lethargic and eat grass.

When the donkey blows his horn, it's time to house your hay and corn. Fish have another way of forecasting the same. When they are biting eagerly and sport near the surface this heralds bad weather.

The clamorous croaking of frogs is a sign of rain. It's the same if the hens in the barnyard are "curling up and pecking."

When the glow-worm lights her lamp,
the air is always very damp.

If the guinea hen calls "come back," bad weather is on the way. If swine become restless, if they grunt loudly, jerk their heads, this is a sign of high winds.

Other signs of rain are assured when horses stretch their necks, sniff the air, or gather in the corner of the field. It follows that if mice or rats become restless and squeak, they send the same message.

New Englanders forecast a long hard winter if muskrats are busy in erecting their homes along the brooks in great numbers and of greater size. They look for the same if the coats of foxes are heavy and they believe a frost will come six weeks after one hears the first katydid.

Look for a hard winter when oysters bed deep, if a rabbit's fur is thick or squirrels store in a large supply of nuts.

A screeching owl signals a storm and pigeons flying in a circle over a body of water prophesy rain.

Unusual activity of ants is another sign of rain. Before a storm they appear in great activity carrying their eggs from place to place. If before eleven in the morning the ants clear their holes and pile the dirt high, this is a sign of fair weather. Stepping on an ant is also believed to bring rain. Also when ants travel in a straight line, expect rain. When they scatter expect fair weather.

Wild geese, wild geese, ganging out to sea
All good weather it will be.

The migration southward or westward of geese in greater numbers in autumn indicates a hard winter ahead; to the north, a siege of hot weather. A gull flying inland reveals a brewing storm; flying toward the open sea, the return of fair weather.

Wind or rain is approaching if gnats bite more and if they fly near the ground or assemble under trees. If they move about gingerly in the open air at evening it is a sign of heat.

Spider webs floating at an autumn sunset bring a night frost. Cobwebs in the grass mean rain before nightfall.

The following attempts to summarize the chapter in rhyme

Beastly Weather

While not inclined to brag or boast
Predicting weather animals are foremost
Listen to what they have to say
Forecasting in a combination of display

When bees to distance wing their flight
Days are warm and skies are bright
But when the flight ends near their home
Stormy weather is sure to come.

When sheep and lambs do gambol and fight,
The weather will change before the night
And when the glow-worm lights her lamp,
The air is invariably cold and damp.

When pigs carry sticks,
The clouds play tricks,
When they lie in the mud
There's no fear of flood

When a cow scratches its ear,
A shower is very near,
If it thumps its rib with a fluffy tail,
Look out for thunder, lightning and hail.

Herd About Town

A rooster crowing on the fence
Predicts rain will come hence.
Found crowing on the ground
Rain surely will come down.

When the peacock loudly bawls,
Soon you'll have both rain and squalls
And if the cock crows before he goes to bed,
He's sure to rise with a watery head

When plovers do fast appear,
It shows that frost is very near,
But when the plovers thus do go,
It time to look for heavy snow.

When the donkey blows his horn,
It's time to house your hay and corn.
When you see gossamer flying.

Ants are All Over

Here is proof of how it once was in our country. It was a time when immigrants came to add to our society instead of arrogantly supplanting to get on the dole. I am not adamant on the point but neither hesitant in relating the story.

A good example, Anthony Santiago, arrived from Antwerp, Belgium; he became a very important contributor to our society, as a result of his penchant for inventions. Anthony is responsible for a pantheon of medical developments including an antiseptic that rendered many malignant diseases dormant and an anti-depressant that has become internationally known.

Anthony created a safety lantern for use in anthracite mines, a sextant that received worldwide acclaim, and he helped perfect a disinfectant for commercial use.

His other discoveries included a bullet proof canteen that military forces all over the world are using. He also developed an antenna for a local power plant that is being distributed nationwide. He remains a consultant for the manufacturer. Anthony is currently working on a new design for a fire hydrant that uses a new propellant to double the water output while keeping a constant pressure.

Innovation runs in the Santiago family. Anthony is a distant descendant and confidant of Anton Antonelli, the famous and gallant anti-aircraft expert from Canton, Ohio, who had a fantastic career in aviation. It was Anton who encouraged Anthony to come to our country.

Hitting our shores in baggy pantaloons and a torn shirt he had only scant funds. Anthony became an occupant in a shanty outside of Chantilly, Virginia. The structure sat a vacant lot. Despite these less than enchanted surroundings, Anthony was mindful of all that went on around him and immediately involved himself in activity.

He planted a large garden introducing new crops to the area including eggplant, cantaloupe, and currants. As a result of his vigilant approach his experiment produced such luxuriant quantities, that he was able to earn money selling his surplus to local merchants.

During the winter months Anthony tried his hand as an anthropologist assistant and worked for the Appellant Court filling a position vacated by the retirement of Manti Mantlo. He was awarded the position over three other applicants.

During this early period Anthony was more than a nonchalant observant of religious history. He was reported to be celebrant at the time, a part of his Protestant upbringing. He gave a new slant to this concept in an elegant talk on virtue. Following his presentation he was a participant in the pursuit of the goal to dismantle prejudice. His confidant manner in believing it would be triumphant moved the program at a rapid pace. His work with pedantic is well documented.

Anthony was never hesitant to take a stand. He was cognizant of the advantage of speaking out to spread his message. It was irrelevant, he lamented, that a tyrant from time to time would have a different view. "We must be tolerant of the ideas of others," he said (his gigantic size helped make the point).

Anthony's claim to fame was interrupted by a call to military service. He served in the infantry as a lieutenant and his flamboyant leadership earned him instant recognition. He was unfortunately wounded by enemy gunfire. Luckily his canteen prevented the bullet from doing significant harm. During his convalescence he studied anthropology more seriously and drafted his plans for improvement for the bullet proof container that would become one of his famous inventions.

After his military career, Anthony met Samantha Cantrell. He was an escort at her debutante party and was instantly impressed by her pleasant manner, and brilliant radiance. He wanted to see more of her. The passionate juices flowing led to a romantic courtship. The desire to right the world gave in to the relationship and they were married.

Several months later they were exuberant to learn Samantha was expectant with child. Several months after she became pregnant, the couple moved into an antebellum mansion which had been dormant for several years. They dismantled much of the main structure. During the remodeling they lived in the tenant house that had been the servant's quarters during the hay day of the property. Samantha was content with the arrangement knowing Anthony was on his way to a successful career and busied herself with renovations and raising the family.

The blessed event came in the middle of the alterations. The nursery, in the recently completed atrium was barely completed. The infant took the name of Anton in memory of Mr. Antonelli, whose picture was proudly displayed over the mantle.

Things moved substantially ahead with the renovations. Among the improvements were a new pantile roof, an expanded pantry, a hand painted mural in the anteroom, and new siding. Many antiques were obtained to grace the changes and the grounds were restored to their earlier plantation appearance, pursuant to a plan from earlier drawings. The remnant they had purchased was taking shape. Some thought the changes were extravagant but, the thought was insignificant to the Santiago family. They knew they had made the right move.

Everything was in place for Anthony to concentrate on his inventions and Samantha to mold Anton into a good inhabitant. You may be assured he was raised with discipline. Any ranting and raving or tantrum throwing was handled immediately. Anthony and Samantha were appreciative of their abundant good fortune and conversant with the role their steady hard work played in its attainment. They are model citizens.

Granted things have changed but, that's the way it used to be with immigrants to America. Want was filled by toil not fantasy and blatant disregard for results from effort. It is more than semantics to suggest that in the "old days" there was no Santa Claus.

Christmas Animals

Mary riding on a donkey, a flock watching by night, cattle lowing, sheep and lamb in the manger, and camels carrying wise men with gold, frankincense and myrrh; truly animals played a vital role at the birth of Christ.

Seven swans a swimming, six geese a-laying, four calling birds, three French hens, two turtle doves, and a partridge in a pear tree. The "Twelve Days of Christmas" also pays tribute to the animal kingdom during the season.

There is however, little debate about who holds the most prestigious position today when it comes to animal influence on Christmas. Santa really knew what he was doing when he selected reindeer to transport all his gifts on Christmas Eve. It wasn't always that way; until the nineteenth century, as St. Nicholas, he had ridden a donkey, a horse, and in a sky chariot drawn by horses.

Traveling the highway of the sky is not for the weak and these animals never reached the status of the coursers from the Arctic. Reindeer are well suited to the North Pole climate. Their body is insulated with a thick coat of long cellular hair, even their ears and nose are furred except for a small bare spot on the tip of the nose. The hoof of the reindeer is also especially adapted to getting around in snow and ice (as well as rooftops).

Other animals have significance at Christmas. Many creatures join in the celebration all over the world. It is fascinating to learn the number of parts they play in the pageant of this festive season.

Camels represent the religious traditions of the season in at least Spain, Mexico, Argentina, Brazil, and Puerto Rico. Children are told that camels carry the Three Kings with their gifts. The youngsters remember the camels, putting out hay or grass for them under their beds, on the roof, or before the door.

In southern Syria the youngest Camel himself bestows the gifts. According to a Syrian Christmas tale, when the young camel was too weary to walk farther, he fell down, and was blessed by the Christ Child. Children awaiting the camels never see them any more than we see the reindeer, but they wake up to find gifts in place of the hay or grass.

At Christmas, peasants of central Europe feed their hens and geese wheat that has been blessed at church, to protect the animals from evil. In some areas the last sheaf of corn at the harvest is dressed like a woman-Corn Mother. On Christmas Eve, a wreath made from the ears of the mother sheaf is put in the manger to assure the cattle thrive.

In recognition of their presence at the birth of the Holy Babe, the people of Scandinavian countries place a sheaf of grain on a tall pole in the dooryard so that the birds may have a happy Christmas. The farm beasts are carefully tended, and the cattle are given extra fodder.

In Sweden the peasants believe that if a spray of mistletoe is hung in a horse's stall, the trolls, or evil creatures will be powerless to injure the beast. Swedes serve "Lussekatter," or "Lucia cats" as a symbol of good luck, since the cat is supposed to keep the devil away.

In Switzerland and some parts of Germany, Christmas Eve is a time when the farmer's wife makes the rounds of the hen house to clip the chicken's wings. It is thought clipping their wings keeps the chickens from flying away and is supposed to protect them against the beasts of prey. In Belgium, the barnyard fowls are given oats that have been blessed for the same purpose.

Also in Belgium, young wrens are said to return at mid-night on Christmas Eve to the nest where they were born. Another of their ancient legends states that during the fourteen days before Christmas there was a great calm on the ocean because the halcyon, or kingfisher, built its nest on the waves and hatched out its young. These were known as the "halcyon days." John Milton describes them in his "Ode on the Morning of Christ's Nativity."

In Spain people show special kindness to their cows at Christmas. They believe that on the Holy Night the cattle breathed upon the Christ child to keep him warm. Another narrative reports the robin's breast is red, because he fluttered his little wings to quicken the dying fire which had been built to warm the Christ Child as he lay in the manger. As the fire grew brighter, the feathers on the robin's breast caught the glow from the flames and have remained red ever since.

In Italy the ceremony is taken to the barn. The farmer and his shepherd carry lighted candles into every corner of the animal's shelter, holding the tapers high, so that light is shed into every dark corner.

Albanians give the first Christmas meat-cake to the house dog as a sign of the sympathy which people believe animals have with the Nativity. In France the custom is to give each house cat all that it can possibly eat on Christmas Eve.

Many believe bees were in attendance at The Birth and to this day they are said to sing in their hives on the night before Christmas. In old England a spray of holly was placed on the hive to wish the bees a Merry Christmas. In other parts of England the popular belief is that sheep walk in procession on Christmas Eve. They do this because the glad tidings of the birth of Christ were first announced by shepherds.

Spiders are even a part of the story. One account has them finding a Christmas tree all trimmed and waiting. In their eagerness to see the pretty things that hung from the branches, they crawled over it from top to bottom, leaving their little grey webs behind. When the Christ Child came to bless the tree and found it hung with spider webs, in order that the mother might not be disappointed when she saw the state of the tree she had so carefully trimmed, he touched the grey webs and turned them to gleaming threads of gold.

Another old European legend says that on Christmas morning oxen are always found on their knees. This is in imitation of the ox and ass that were in the manger and knelt when Christ was born. They are supposed to be given the power of speech during that one night, but woe to the person who listens to them talk, for death is supposed to find him before seven days have passed.

German peasants think that if a dog howls the night before Christmas it will go mad within a year. Little girls are told that if they eat no beans on Christmas Eve they will become a donkey. It is also thought that if you dream of a black cat on Christmas Eve you will suffer a serious illness.

On a more pleasant note, the story of animals at Christmas ends with a carol that summarizes the story.

The Friendly Beasts
(A 12th Century English Carol)

Jesus our brother, strong and good,
Was humbly born in a stable rude,
And the friendly beasts around Him stood,
Jesus our brother, strong and good.

"I," said the donkey, shaggy and brown,
"I carried His mother up hill and down,

"I carried her safely to Bethlehem town;
"I," said the donkey, shaggy and brown.

"I," said the cow all white and red,
"I gave Him my manger for His bed,
"I gave Him my hay to pillow His head,
"I," said the cow all white and red.

"I," said the sheep with curly horn,
"I gave Him my wool for His blanket warm,
"He wore my coat on Christmas morn;
"I," said the sheep with curly horn.

"I," said the dove, from the rafters high,
"Cooed Him to sleep, my mate and I,
"We cooed Him to sleep, my mate and I;
"I," said the dove, from the rafters high.

And every beast, by some good spell,
In the stable dark was glad to tell,
Of the gift he gave Immanuel,
The gift he gave Immanuel.

Animals appearing in Christmas Animals.

Bee
Birds
Camel
Cat
Cattle
Chicken
Cow
Dog
Donkey
Geese
Hen

Herd About Town

Horse
Lamb
Oxen
Partridge
Reindeer
Sheep
Spider
Swan
Turtledove
Wren

Flightless Birds

Scientists have found the fossil remains of reptile-like birds that lived over 125,000,000 years ago. They are commonly called "Archaeopteryx," the ancient one with wings.

A bird is able to fly because of the shape of its wings and feathers. A wing has only three fused digits (perhaps developed from the ancient pentadactyl); it is actually a modified arm. Like an airplane, a bird's wing in flight is flat on the bottom and slightly rounded on top. This shape is called an "airfoil" in plane design. It creates a difference in air pressure above and below, which gives the wing the necessary "hoist."

To become airborne, a bird springs upward on its strong legs, extends its feathered wings at the same time and flaps them rapidly. Consequently, a "lift" phenomenon takes over and the bird takes flight. The wing is extremely light because the bones are thin, and hollow. They also can be neatly folded back next to the body when not in use.

The feathers of birds flow out from the skin, like the hairs of mammals. Long flight feathers grow from the forearm, while smaller contour feathers grow from the top of the wing, making a smooth surface, which lets the air flow easily over the wing in flight. Birds normally have a breastbone with a large ridge that looks and works like the keel that runs along the bottom of a sailboat.

Non-flying birds do not have this ridge for the attachment of the wing muscles. Their breast bones are gently curved, more like the bottom of a raft. The scientific name for this flightless class is ratitae, or ratites, from the Latin word meaning raft. The bones of ratites are also much heavier than those of birds that fly. Birds that fly have a Y-shaped bone in front of the breast bone that we sometimes call the wishbone. Ratites do not have wishbones.

The history of ratites has many interesting details as discussed below.

Shortly after its discovery, New Zealand was nicknamed by zoologist "Ornithogea," the continent of birds. It was not because it contained more species than anywhere else, but because birds were the highest form of life to have evolved on the island. Because they did not have to take to the air to escape predators or build nests in trees, out of the reach of rodents, the birds of New Zealand gradually lost the power of flight.

As a result, they were largely defenseless when the Polynesians arrived in the 14th century. The dogs and the stowaway rats brought in Polynesian canoes decimated the earthbound birds. Many species became extinct; others retreated to remote parts of the island. Some survived by developing defensive skills such as speed, kicking and swimming ability, fighting expertise, and concealment strategies.

Perhaps the best known of the ratite is the ostrich. It is also the largest ratite, in fact, it is the largest of all birds, weighing in many cases over 300 lbs. The ostrich often travels with zebras and antelope and does a good job keeping up. Despite its size it can run at speeds up to 50 mph. Contrary to popular belief the ostrich does not hide its head in the sand. Sometimes it lies on the ground resting or eating, giving the appearance its head is in the sand.

A lesser-known of the non-flyers is the rhea. A close relative, it resembles the ostrich but is smaller. It has three toes on each foot, (the ostrich has two), has large wings, and grows to a height of about 5 feet weighing up to 50 lbs. The rhea usually lives in flocks of 20 to 30 birds, generally in brush-covered land near water where they can bathe and swim. The rhea makes its home in South America.

Another non-flyer, the cassowary, has a massive body, long legs and a featherless neck and head. A bone helmet known as a casque-usually blue-used for butting through the undergrowth covers the head. The cassowary grows up to 5-feet tall weighing up to 120 lbs. They can run up to 40 miles an hour and can leap 6-feet or more in the air with ease. Each foot has three toes armed with sharp claws that are deadly weapons in a fight. The cassowary is a flightless tank with steel nerves.

Australia's national bird, the Emu, is also unable to take to the skies. Standing 5 to 6-feet high and weighing in the neighborhood of 100 pounds doesn't help (only the ostrich is taller). Emu's usually have thick feathers and long legs. Their wings are so small that they are mere stubs.

The Kakapo also fits into the Ratite class. This rare New Zealand parrot, known also as owl parrot or night kaka and ground parrot or burrowing parrot, has fairly well-developed wings, but it is so heavy (reaching 50 lbs.) it is incapable of true flight.

A further peculiarity of this parrot concerns the powerful booming calls of the males. The males gather in a restricted area and proceed to boom for 45-seconds, uttering one boom every 3-seconds; they then fall silent for 45-seconds before starting up again.

New Zealand is also the home of the kiwi bird, a shy and seldom seen grounded bird. About the size of a chicken it has a stocky body covered with shaggy, dull brown feathers. Its neck and legs are short, and its bill is long and flexible. The kiwi has no tail, and its wings are tiny and useless. Their claws occupy the space where wings would normally be; great for defense but not much for getting in the air.

The kiwi female lays eggs that are up to 1/3 of the mother's body weight. No other bird lays such a large egg in proportion to its body size. The kiwi is also the only bird with nostrils at the tip of its bill, used to smell food in the thick forests where it lives.

Although not a ratite, the penguin is a member of the non-flying brigade. Penguins lost the ability to fly millions of years ago and remain the only flightless diving bird. The penguin's wing developed into flippers, which serve as paddles, working in harmony with their web feet. They have modified eyes for seeing under water. Penguins can reach speeds up to 40-mph in the water. Dense feathers form a waterproof coat, thick layers of fat keep them warm in cold water. Penguins only come to shore to reproduce.

South America has several Grebes that cannot fly. Usually named for the lakes where they are found, many are on the verge of extinction. Most eat their own feathers. It is theorized that the mat of feathers found in their stomachs acts as a buffer to prevent fish bones from entering the intestines until they are soft enough to digest.

Lesser-known classes round out the ratite clan. These include the Takake, a large marsh bird, the flightless cormorant, found on the Galapagos Island, and the Wekas, a resident of New Zealand.

Ratites eat anything. Items such as watches, bottle caps, glass, locks, and alarm clocks have been found in their stomachs. No need to feel sorry for this class. What would seem at first glance to be a great disadvantage for a bird turns out to be a motivation for adaptability. Perhaps there is a good lesson for us all to keep in mind. Bloom where you're planted is their message.

Animals appearing in Flightless Birds.

Bird
Cassowary
Chicken
Cormorant
Dogs
Emu
Kakapo
Night keka
Ostrich
Owl
Parrot
penguin
Ratitites
Rhea
Riva
Takake
Wekan

Crazy Farm

You never know where we might turnip. Last summer we spent a few days of our vacation at one of the most unusual farms. Peas lettuce tell you about it.

The Porterhouse, wasn't in what you would call mint condition. It had been in the Moss family for almost a century and really needed sprucing up. It wasn't eggsactly what we wanted, actually the rooms were a shambles and the yard was a mess.

When we arrived the farmer's wife was in the mushroom fixing lunch. Our approach for accommodations was at first met with a leaf me alone attitude. Finally, we were led to our room. A nap sack hung over the bed post and hogwash was hanging from the clothesline. No wonder it was dirt cheap.

We later met the proprietor. He was as big as a horse. He had a whale of an appetite; ate like a pig, could really wolf it down. Although he looked pasta his prime he had a reputation as a night owl. No wonder he took cat naps all day. No spring chicken, he could still cut the mustard, so they say.

Exploring the area, we found an ax was mounted on a chopstick; wheat was shredded about the area. The pond was alive with activity. A school of fish was loud at recess, frogs croaked a bass note in support of the bird's song and the ducks paddled in unison. A goose almost gagged yelling "take a gander at those fools," as a snake slithered by in the sunlight.

The goats bucked the trend and headed for the dump and the pigs went off to the market squealing. The owl didn't give a hoot and the wolves were heard howling in the distance as the parrot mocked all parties, as if it were a ventriloquist.

Hens laid eggplant and fowl balls, hiding them under a rock using a hatchet. Cows were no longer content and stayed in a bad mood. It was udder turmoil as they were used to living in conditions more like camel lot.

The lambs had been fleeced but were quiet about it, as ewe might expect. The sheep were sheer naked. The wolver wine got intoxicated. Thank goodness the skunk had become extinct.

The owner's dog, a melancholy, chased the pigeon toed cat that had littered the porch. We saw a robin robbing a worm. The mules bayed at the moon. The only stable member of the farm was the stallion who showed some horse sense staying away from these weird characters.

The crops at this place were also in disarray, I never saw anything to beet it. The celery was bloodshot claiming to have been in a rhubarb, after being collard by the Swiss chard. The cucumbers were in a sour mood; they stayed in a pickle. The tomatoes turned red with rage and the carrots were green with envy as the corn flaked to heights unknown.

Grapes openly worried about raisin their young in such an environment, it was the pits. Squash were crushed about the conditions and ended up with a strawberry fighting with the sweet potato that was in a rutabaga mood. Beans snapped their disapproval.

Apples had formed a core to combat the problems, but the idea got shot down. The chives picked up the battle with the endive but the garlic and onion teamed up bringing tears to the group with their a peal. Spinach peppered the cress and arti-choked the asparagus. The pumpkin who didn't mince words, told them he thought they were all crazy.

What an experience. We were naturally glad to conclude our visit but have since decided we would lichen to return one day. Weir considering doing it again in the near future. Do you think we're nuts? Care to come along?

Animals appearing in Crazy Farm.

Bird
Cow
cow
Dog
dove
Fish
Frog
Goat
Goose
Hen
Horse
Lamb

Mule
Owl
Parrot
Pig
Pigeon
Sheep
Skunk
Snake
Whale
Wolf
Wolverine
Worm

Noah's Ark

Where the Term Poop-Deck Originated.

Listen buoys and gulls to the story of how animals had fun on a boat ride many years ago as reported in the *National Henquirer.* Once upon a time there was an ark that sailed into the Purrsian gulf. The cargo was a group of animals who cast their bred upon the waters. Under a noah-it-all captain, the stock was floated in an effort to profit from their multiplying.

The scheme was under the guidance of the captain's chief investi-gator, crankie crocodile. Before using his professional advice the captain made many mistakes. He had a ten antcy to put the cart before the horse, which really served no apparent porpoise. He spent his time making cuff lynx for the passengers. He amused himself further by locking bees in the ark-hives. He spent hours listening to them hum his favorite tune; "Won't You Bee My honey." He had a wife that didn't help matters. She went stork raving mad after the birth of their 10th child.

There was unrest on the ship as apes practiced guerilla warfare and played King Kong war games. There really was no cause for alarm since the only ammunition they had was home-made meringue-a-tan pie. They were considered blab-boons as a result of their ongoing chatter and fake warfare.

The rabbits lived in hare-raid shelters, concerned what the apes might try next. This division gave them ample time to multiply, adding substantially to their numbers. This activity did not subtract from their ingenuity. They built little hutch back cars and drove them all over the ship ram ming them into each other; trying to out fox one another. The winner always crowed about his accomplishments. Their cunning even helped develop a miniature rabbit transit system built especially for one-horse-power use.

Horses raced about the track on their own power. The annual mare-athon on this course was won by the same stallion every year. This stud trained by playing stable tennis every-day. He was very popular with the fillies and kept a steady pace in his grooming habits, which some said was his mane asset.

His sister, Whinny, an animated filly, was featured in the center foal of *Herd About Town.* Harry equine, their father was fur-ious, telling her "that's the last straw, you've broken the family gait, hit the trail."

Whiny floundered around for a while and ended up playing bit parts in horse shows. Despite her slow start she rallied to become a leading performer. She stared in many winning films before settling down, marrying a galloping gilding. He was a Kentucky hat contender who went on to win 2- parts of the tribal crown held on an Arizona Indian reservation (what else can a gelding do).

Chickens roosted at the annual assembly formed to keep law and order. Their rights were represented by E. G. G. Hatch who was voted "the top chicken libber" of the year, when he won the case of getting better living conditions for his clients.

Hatch was also successful in recouping restitution for the fowl treatment the chickens received in the past. He achieved these accomplishments by poaching on the doorstep of the members of the council. He was egged on by the entire flock, all of whom had an assigned tusk to assist in the effort. A definite pecking order was established and those who couldn't hatchet-it were given the ax and sent to join the mislaid eggs.

Stags were also well represented in this legislative body. Their lobbyist was Fawn Doe. She was a deer, and over many years gained the reputation for not passing the buck. Her motto "the buck stops here", although often misunderstood, was very effective in the long run.

Snakes aboard the ark went into hiss-terics when they learned Noah was going to use them as windshield vipers. Oh well, you can't venom all! Not wanting to make an asp of themselves they went off in adder confusion calculating it was better to be out of sight. They slithered from deck to deck trying to worm out of the appointed task. The presence of the mongoose helped to prevent too much complaining from them. They really weren't the type to grab the tiger by the tail.

The hyenas laughed all the time, always complaining about time flying when they were having fun. We don't even have time to duck out and get ostracized, they would say. They would quack everyone up with the many stories they related.

Only a phew skunks were on the vessel and they weren't very popular. They smelled like dragon breath. Their behavior was out of odor most of the time. No one hounded them. Even the turtles with their built in escape hatch avoided them.

Entertainment was available on the voyage in many forms. Cats listened to mewsic. Buffalo roamed the deck stampeding to the harmonizing of the bear-i-tone lions (a bit auk ward but amusing). Dragons let off steam as camouflage for lizards as they leaped about the dance floor in their bare mid-drifts. Minnie the mermaid, a deep she fish, would sing "roc around the croc" by the hour. Bees seemed to enjoy her act the most but, became too affectionate for her liking. She finally told them to" bug off honey" and said if they didn't stop mis-bee-hiving she would turn them over to the sting operation for pun-ishment.

The emcee was usually Ele Phant from Tuscaloosa. He also played the piano tickling the ivories with the best of them. During his performance he talked mumbo jumbo but, he remembered every song he ever played. When things got out of hand, crabs played policeman, and pinched the offenders.

Oxen were the handymen of the crew being yak of all trades. They were very talented making fish and chip-indale reproductions out of dogwood. They sold them for a lark.

Pigs were thought of as real boars. They took everything for grunted and would try to hog all the food. Until one hot day at a picnic one exclaimed "I never sausage heat, I'm almost bacon. The pigs were conscious if they didn't change their ways they could end up being the picnic. Some hogs had trouble with warts (wart hogs) and others were hamstrung but they all had fun.

The insects were ill much of the time, living on ant-i-bodics. Donkeys also experienced poor health living on burro'd time. Both spent a great amount of time in the waspital.

Dogs were overweight, because of their eating habits, always taking a second yelping. They really pigged out. They could wolf it down and you never heard them bitch when there was food around. On occasion they were observed squirreling away the meals of others in a doggy bag.

A frog broke his leg and had to be toad to his room. He recovered quickly leaping back to jumping status in a tad.

Fish had a reel good time going to school. They swam upstream to learn. Starting on a small scale, they mastered how to travel in carp pools. They studied Finnish, played "salmon says" and "carps and robbers." They bought their own supplies paying for them with credit cods. On a scale of 1 to 10 their life was about a 5 but they held the line and vowed to remain in the race until there was a sole survivor. It was speculated that would be rock codzilla, the meanest of them all, or captain squid who had even more gull than rock.

Swordfish had a duel personality but, were good students. While on the ship they took advance courses on King Arthur and his knights in an effort to become more effective with their natural asset. Catfish nearly drowned chasing mice underwater. One had to be recovered by C. P. R. Swim, who also gave him an exercise program to regain proper mussel tone.

Birds worked diligently making sparrow chutes that doubled as sails when needed. They also spent a lot of time telling stories. Their favorites were marine tales such as "fighting marines" and "lobster tails" (once upon a time there was a lobster). it was considered a cardinal sin to tell any off color yarns. They would badger everyone trying to pigeon-hole them with their tails. Most everyone agreed they could really louse up a day and would leap frog over everything to avoid them.

Whales were known as blubber -mouths as they flaunted their knowledge of the moby-dick-ionary. They also relished chewing blubber gum but couldn't stomach Jonah who they claimed always spouted off without knowing what he was talking about. All in all they had a people of a good time.

Shrimp lived on cocktails and consequently fell a lot. They clammed it was because they were accident prawn. Mayflies gave the passengers a hard time. They were very annoying always buzzing in a bragging manner about the seafaring experiences they had aboard the Aprilflower.

The chief lobsteritrican reported on births during the voyage. Cows had heifer dozen offspring. Holy cow! It's udderly amazing what a little jerk can do. The fodder of the brood was very helpful cowoperating with his wife Bessie in raising the young. He was often seen playing moos-ical chairs with them, taking them to the moos-eum and teaching them manners. It was from him they learned to say thank ewe. On Saturday you would be sure to find the whole family at the moo-vies.

Bossy, the dad, was also instrumental in introducing the kids to such publications as *Cows-mopolitan* and *Breeders Digest*. Despite the fact they knew the cub reporter personally, they weren't allowed to read the daily newspaper. Both parents agreeing that no moos was good moos,

Following the unusual number of births a survey was conducted which produced the following conclusions. Nervous cows make milk shakes, pampered cows give spoiled milk, and forgetful cows have milk of amnesia offspring.

The goats and sheep got together without supervision having predictable results. One young was reported to have the ability to eat tin cans and give back steel wool. Billy Baa, the father of the children, saw the enterprising value of the kid and formed a corporation. The product became so popular that the family was listed in "Ewe Who." There was a time you could keep track of the firm's progress daily through the "Wool Street Journal" but, unfortunately things went a fowl.

The company's production formula was stolen by a crook who shepherded the idea with a couple of changes to the underground where two moles ran the business tunneling the product to port using the well established beaver express. The former owners were sheepish about pressing charges, thinking they would be embarrassed by this "pull the wool over your eyes" escapade. The thieves continued to prosper.

The tortoise couldn't keep a secret, telling everything they learned through the ape vine. Monkeys were a chimp off the old block. They swung from vine to vine playing funny games. The passengers would often exclaim, "take a gander at those buzzards they soar like a hawk. Where do they get all that energy?"

Peacocks strutted around all day looking pretty, trying to catch the eagle's eye. Last report had them making little progress. The eagle showing an I don't caribou you impression. The aggravation would make them soar.

Cranes never lifted their head to do anything, going out of their way to duck anything resembling work. When Noah called for volunteers they were quiet as a mouse, not moving a mussel.

It's hard to believe there was so much activity with the ship so full. Being packed in like sardines may have intensified the adventure. Whatever the case it is unlikely a trip with so much hustle bustle will ever take place again. Time to seal off.

Animals appearing in Noah.

ant
ape
asp
badger
bear
bee
bird

boar
buck
buffalo
bug
buzzard caribou
cardinal
carp
cat
catfish
chicken
cows
crab
crocodile
deer
doe
dog
dragon
elephant
fish
flea
fly
frog
goat
gorilla
gull
hog
horse, equine, gilding, filly, mane, mare, stag, stallion, stud
hyena
kangaroo
lark
lizard
lobster
lynx
mice
moles
mongoose
monkey

mouse
mussel
oxen
pawn
peacock
pig
pigeon
porpoise
rabbit
ram
seal
sheep
shrimp
skunk
snakes
sparrow
squid
stork
tiger
tortoise
turtle
warthog
wasp
whale
yak

Pardon the intrusion of Mother Nature. The rhyme below won't qualify for a poetry award but hopefully will stimulate some different thoughts about this lady that plays such an important role in our life and that of animals. Note the similarity of features and traits.

Mother Nature and Me

Some think it to be untrue
Not many would pursue
Hear the story of Mother Nature and me
How we learned to live in harmony

Not to evaluate whether this rhyme is good
Concentrate on the content if you would
Stay with it and if you endure
You'll see another side of nature

Overlook the spelling, hope you'll pardon
A heart has a beet, so does a garden
Cars, trees and elephants all have trunks
But they wouldn't make scents for skunks

Nature's slug is a slimy thing
Mine will make your ears ring
Her cranes fly on the wing
For mine lifting is their thing

Her sky has a ceiling her ocean a floor
My lion (lying) distasteful hers has a roar
My mouse clicks, hers squeaks
Her hare has fur, mine streaks

Her cricket chirps, mine is a game
It's no bull they're not the same
A large variance in our croc

Herd About Town

Both ugly, neither worthy of mock

Her crow flies, mine is a brag
My going alone unlike her stag
Her duck waddles, mine goes underneath
Her hen peck unlike mine, it has teeth

My calf has a leg, hers is a cow
My dogs hurt, hers bow-wow
My creek in the bones, hers has a flow
My deer is a spouse, hers is a doe

I have a front she does as well
My wave is handy hers a swell
Her wind can kick up a storm
For me hot air is the norm

Her quagmire and mine about the same
Comparison of watershed may be lame
Mine a function of discharge
Hers an accumulation, an enlarge

Giving presents I have a buy-you
Not as pleasant murky, runs her bayou
Land and water similar is a swamp
Not a good place to romp

My basin is porcelain shaped like a bowl
Hers formed by glaciers out of control
My brush paints, hers is a bush
Also a difference in our blush

The goose is another bone of contention
Hers with feathers, mine human invention
Another difference that's profound
My afghan a cover, hers a hound

Other things common in nature and me
The sun supplies us both with energy
Too bad we are not more the same
Not my choice; for change I am game

Ever since I was a little tike
I wished we were more alike

Animals appearing in Mother Nature and Me.

afghan
bull
calf
cow
Crane
cricket
crocodile
crow
deer
doe
dpg
duck
Elephant
goose
hare
hen
lion
mouse
Skunk
Slug
stag

Animals in Politics

Loyal, friendly, cuddly, faithful, devoted, dutiful and cute are terms you are likely to encounter to describe our pets and other animal friends. While many of us have been "fleeced" by politicians, normally you wouldn't think of animals as the bureaucratic type, but you will find them in many precincts of government. Some play key roles and have important influence on our political system. No bull.

Known for its' gentleness and purity, the dove is recognized as the international symbol for peace and the aggressive hawk as its opposite. The donkey and the elephant have been long term representatives of the democratic and republican parties and the eagle reigns as our national insignia as well as being found in many emblems. A variety of other animals participate in the political process.

The heraldry of our nation shows a real affection for the animal kingdom. The eagle is found on the flags of Iowa, Illinois, Michigan, New York, North Dakota, and Utah. Michigan adds an elk and a moose, and Utah has a beehive. Buffalo emerge on Wyoming's pennant and are joined by eagle feathers on Oklahoma's standard bearer. California uses a bear, Missouri has two. Horses prance on Pennsylvania's flag and pull a plow on South Dakota's. Louisiana features a pelican and the badger is highlighted by the Wisconsin banner.

Our justice system refers to a court that ignores principles of justice; a court characterized by incompetence and dishonesty; as a kangaroo court. The kangaroo plays an additional role being the explanation for a ticket in which the candidate for vice president is more popular than the candidate for President.

Appropriations made for projects that are not essential, but are sought because they pump money and resources into the local district of the sponsoring legislator, are referred to as pork barrel legislation. Is this another "pig in a poke" scheme?

Among other choice "pet" names candidates for office and office holders are referred to as dark horses, also rans, and lame ducks.

The animals nominated as political representatives were not always elected hands (or Paws) down. Let's take a look at some of the races and a few of the uncontested predicaments that led to their appointments.

The selection of the dove, as the symbol of peace, was probably connected to Noah's Ark (Genesis 8:8-12) telling of the dove returning with the olive branch of peace between God and man. Therefore, one who prefers talking rather than fighting (especially in international conflicts) is called a dove.

The eagle almost didn't make it as a national symbol. How would you like to have a turkey as your national representative? That's what Benjamin Franklin wanted. When others suggested an eagle because eagles have traditionally been symbols of power, Franklin objected. He said they had "bad moral character" because they stole food from weaker birds. On the other hand, he said, "The turkey is in comparison a much more respectable bird, a true original native of America." Congress eventually chose the bald eagle, which is found only in North America.

The Democratic Donkey started its leadership role in 1870. The popular Harpers Weekly cartoonist Thomas Nast drew "a live jackass kicking a dead lion." The sketch had the U.S. Capitol building and the U.S. eagle in the background. The carcass was generally understood to be the Secretary of War Edwin M. Stanton and the donkey the treacherous Copperheads (the Northern backers of the Southern cause at the time of the Civil War).

The Democrats and other Copperhead opponents loved the cartoon. The donkey became permanently associated with the Democratic Party, even though it was used mostly as a sign of ridicule against them. The Democrats decided to use the donkey as their symbol and turn the ridicule to their own advantage. Adding still another animal to the fold, boll weevils became the nickname for the Southern Democrats.

The Republican Elephant had a similar beginning to the donkey of the opposition. In 1874 Nast drew another cartoon, for the same publication, which suggested a Republican figure to the public. The drawing showed wooden boards, which were platform planks, being thrown everywhere by an out-of-control elephant labeled the Republican vote. The cartoon also included a donkey in a lion's skin, which was immediately recognizable to most of the magazine's readers as the Democratic Party. Like the Democrat's donkey, the elephant was not intended as a complimentary symbol at first, but it caught on and has remained with the Grand Old Party. Both may in a sense be considered dark horses (see below).

Much is written today about candidates. What would reporters do without animal terms too pave the way for their descriptions? Many stories originate from speeches on the rubber chicken circuit, a name given to functions where the menu offerings are the least important part of the program. All the way to and including the inauguration, critters are used to explain status and actions of candidates and officeholders.

The term dark horse is traced to a Tennessee horse trader who owned an extremely fast black stallion. He made a practice of riding the horse into a strange town as though it were an ordinary saddle horse and then persuading the locals to set up a horse race. Not knowing they were up against a proven winner, the townspeople usually lost, and the trader's dark horse became legendary. It's easy to see how, the expression made its way into political use.

Staying on the track, we come upon "also rans". In most horse races, judges do not determine the order of finish. They simply clock the first three animals across the line. Newspapers of the last century naturally gave prominence to horses that placed in important races. They frequently described all three animals, gave their time, and listed their owners and winnings. Toward the end of such a story it was customary to mention the horses that-also ran.

During the third quarter of the century, United States presidential elections came to resemble horse races. Many new parties were organized. Their candidates seldom gave any serious competition to men selected by old-line parties, So after elections, newspapers dismissed many an obscure aspirant for the presidency as an also-ran one who didn't come close enough to winning to have his order determined. By the turn of the century the expression had come to be applied to any person badly beaten in competition of any sort.

A lame duck is an officeholder who has lost the election for the next term but still has some time to serve before a successor is inaugurated. One account says the term comes to us from Exchange Alley, eighteenth-century London's equivalent of Wall Street. There, people who couldn't pay their debts were referred to as lame ducks because, it was said, they "waddled out of the Alley." Incidentally, it was here that stockbrokers first divided backers and forecasters into two classes; bulls and bears.

Another lame duck story goes back to Revolutionary times, perhaps earlier. There was a woodsman maxim, "Never waste powder on a dead duck." From that, "dead duck" became popular slang, still in use, for anything-person or article-that is no longer worth a straw, that is done up, played out. Some bright wit a hundred years ago, probably a political writer with that slang term in mind, saw a chance for an apt modification. By the law that then existed (revised but the Twentieth Amendment, February 6, 1933), members of Congress who might fail of re-election in November, nevertheless still held office until March 4th following. Such outgoing "ducks" were not yet “dead", merely "lamed," they could still, if sufficiently numerous, propose and pass legislation embarrassing to an incoming administration.

The word inauguration comes from the word "auger" which in ancient Rome meant someone who foretold the future by observing the flight of birds. Among the many things an augur would do is determine whether or not you should do something by the way the birds were flying. These almost magical soothsayers would tell a general not to march on one day or do battle on another by the formations of the birds on the wing. They might even catch one and cut it open to observe its entrails. An "inauguration" was done before beginning any major venture.

Auspicious also came from this bird study by the ancients. If the birds were flying in the right way, then the day was considered auspicious: a good one in which to start a project. The word literally means "bird watcher.” We all know that some of our politicians are "for the birds" and even “bird-brained,” but you may not have known the history.

Lastly, so as to not leave anyone out, we must give some mention to the weasel words we often hear from our legislative representatives, the red herring issues used to distract the public from the more important issues, the catty politicians who often "dog" their constituents and the paper tiger position papers that flaunt power beyond what is actual. The political arena is a real zoo if not a jungle.

Animals in Politics.

aardvark
alligator
anteater
antelope
armadillo
badger
bear
beaver
Bee
bird
boll weevil
buffalo
bumblebee
camel
caterpillar
chicken
crab
critters
crocodile
dinosaur
dog
dolphin
donkey
dove
dragon
duck

eagle
elephant
elk
fish, herring
giraffe
grub
hare
hawk
horse
horse
kangaroo
lion
lobster
mammoth
mastodon
mole
monkey
moose
octopus
owl
oxen
pelican
pig
pigeon
porcupine
rat
snake,
turkey
turtle
turtle
whale

Games

Animal Crackers

1. What animal are you if you have a cold?
2. What animals are in all banks?
3. What animal is on every legal document?
4. What animal is in every baseball game?
5. What animal needs clothing, poor thing?
6. What animal never plays fair?
7. What animal is nearest your brain?
8. What animal do you need when your driving a car?
9. What animal is your girl-friend?
10. What animal is tiresomely?
11. What animal has the most brains of any?
12. Why is the camel so easily angered?
13. When is a donkey spelled with one letter?
14. What two animals go with you everywhere?
15. What animals do you find in the clouds?
16. What animal would you like to be on a cold day?
17. What farm animal is very much like a cannibal?
18. What animal is the heaviest in all creation?
19. What well-known animal drives an automobile?

Bird Bafflers

1. What bird is a letter?
2. What bird is essential to eating?
3. What bird is a high dignitary of the church*
4. What bird is a chessman?

5. What good bird deserves another?
6. What two birds are foolish?
7. What bird is a name?
8. What bird is getting run over all the time?
9. What bird can lift the heaviest weight?
10. What is the rudest bird?
11. How do we know that nightingales are very gay birds?
12. How do canary birds pay their debts?
13. When is a pigeon like a drinking glass?
14. Which bird is the lowest-spirited?

Common Terms

All of the following have something in common. Can you figure it out?

Barouche
Berlin
Break/brake
Brougham
Buckboard
Buggy
Cabriolet
Calash
Chaise
Clarence/growler
Conestoga wagon
Coupe
Curricle
Disobliged ants
Diligence
Dogcart
Dos-a-doe
Dray
Droshky
Fiacre
Fly
Four-in-hand
Gharry
Gig
Hackney carriage

Hansom
Jaunting car
Phaeton
Post chaise
Quadria
Stanhope
Sulky
Surrey
Tilburg
Tonga
Trap
Troika
Tumbrel
Victoria
Vis-a-vis
Wain

Cows and Gators Riddles

1. What do you get when you cross a cow with a belly dancer?

2. What do you get from a cow that reads the Readers Digest

3. What do you get from a forgetful cow?

4. What do you get form an invisible cow?

5. What do you get from a magician's cow?

6. What do you get from an Alaskan cow?

7. What do you get from a funny cow?

8. What don't cows like to tell jokes?

9. Do cows often graze alone?

10. What alligators love cream cheese on a bagel?

11. What alligators go to church socials?

12. What alligators join the navy?

13. What alligators join the FBI?

14. What alligators prefer old-fashioned phones?

Here are thirty well-known fish, with a good clue given for each one. How many can you catch?

1. What is a struggling fish?
2. What is a cheating fish given to sharp practices?
3. What is a fish of precious metal?
4. What fish is man's best friend?
5. What fish is a royal fish?
6. What is a heavenly fish?
7. What fish is in the band?
8. What fish is an animal that is almost extinct?
9. What fish is an ugly old witch?
10 What fish is a household pet?
11. What fish do you find in a bird cage?
12. What fish is good with hot biscuits?
13. What fish is a sharp-pointed weapon that soldiers used in Robin Hood's time?
14. What fish is a member of a barber shop quartet?
15. What fish is a deep guttural sound?
16. What fish is used on certain boats?
17. What fish is very useful in hot weather?
18. What fish is used by a fencer?
19. What fish is seen at night?
20. What poor fish is always ailing?
21. What fish makes a good sandwich?
22. What fish is a very evil fish?
23. What fish is a very dark color?
24. What fish floats through the air?
25. What fish is a favorite with dairy farmers?
26. What fish is a rosy biter?
27. What fish represents three letters used by stores delivering goods you buy?
28. What fish represents a process used in refining metals?
29. What is a gloomy, down-in-the-mouth fish?
30. What fish warms the earth?

Hink-Pinks

Many have played the following game in one form or another, perhaps not by the name; Hink-Pink. What's different here is that the entries have been constructed to limit the answers to members of the animal kingdom. The directions in the next paragraph will assist you in moving through this zoo.

The left column suggests a clear concise definition for which you must translate into two words that rhyme. The resulting answer will always contain the name of an animal or identify an expression about an animal. The idea is to answer a definition with a rhyming combination of adjective and noun; "funny cat" for instance would be a "witty kitty." Sometimes the answer will be a word repeated (animal blemish=mole mole).

Hink-pinks are often easier to create than to guess, and they are fun at parties-if everyone happens to be in the mood. See how many you can get before turning to the answers.

1. bird cloth
2. bird comb
3 bird conversation
4. bird gulp
5. bird ladle
6. bird language
7. bird longing
8. bird maneuver
9. bird mate
10. bird musician
11. bird prison
12. bird screech
13. bird skirmish

14. bird spool
15. bird stick
16. bird stink
17. bird utensil
18. bird valley
19. bird wince
20. blackbird movie
21. avian radiance
22. crow refuge
23. disgusting bird
24. fast bird
25. reptile barrier
26. gobbler meat
27. damp animal
28. alligator barge
29. antelope Chevrolet
30. antelope collection
31. antelope drum
32. antelope farm
33. antelope female
34. uncommon grizzly
35. rodent knife
36. solitary bee
37. tiny drone
38. uninteresting bird
39. buzzard knowledge
40. grouse auction
41. hawk nip
42. heron remorse
43. proud heron
44. raven radiance
45. seagull head
46. titmouse seizure
47. waterfowl biscuit
48. waterfowl song
49. woodpecker giggle
50. fish cards

51 fish container
52. fish cooking
53. fish cover
54. fish doctor
55. fish march
56. fish tailor
57. fish temple
58. fish throat
59. chic fish
60. midget fish
61. nibbling fish
62. peaceful herring
63. peculiar fish
64. solitary fish
65. evil herring
66. salmon fastener
67. stingy mollusk
68. trout plate
69. toad stump
70. street frog
71 goat governess
72. goose glance
73. geese wiggle
74. untied waterfowl
75. grouse auction
76. grouse shell
77. ape bow
78 ape dirigible
79. ape fighter
80. gorilla garment
81. hawk battle
82. hog hairpiece
83. horse cough
84. horse food
85. horse joke
86 horse pennant
87. horse shedding

88. bogus horse
89. happy horse
90. haughty horseman
91. foolish mare
92. happy whinny
93. sturdy barn
94. throaty mare
95. insect award
96. insect carpet
97. insect embrace
98. insect joint
99. insect merriment
100. insect prescription
101. obese fly
102. animal pageant
103. animal bone
104. lizard stench
105. animal basin
106. animal blemish
107. animal burrow
108. animal psychiatrist
109. ape dirigible
110. elk dessert
111. moth murder
112. mouse part
113. rodent home
114. friendly rodents
115. talkative rodent
116. rodent shoe
117. animal observer
118. pig argument
119. pig news
120. pig wound
121. large porker
122. quality pigs
123. midday raccoon
124. rabbit cash

125. rabbit den
126. rabbit sack
127. rabbit trap
128. humorous rabbit
129. naked rabbit
130. unhip rabbit
131. hare addiction
132. sheep streetcar
133. lamb cry
134. stingy lamb
135. shrimp griddle
136. inebriated animal
137. lug netting
138. slug path
139. cobra pain
140. snake dance
141. snake sigh
142. snake shooter
143. cobra pain
144. rattlesnake fighter
145. reptile drink
146. reptile pole
147. tarantula juice
148. gobbler meat
149. reptile barrier
150. wasp trumpet
151. weasel pest
152. groovy whales
153. crustacean prison

Riddles

1. What two classes is the animal kingdom divided into?

2. What do anteaters like on their pizza?

3. What do nuts chase after with little nets?

4. What is a hibve.*

5. What insect plays football?

6. Where did Noah keep his bees?

7. What do you get if a little bear sits in a corn field?

8. How do matadors write letters?

9. What do you give a sick bird?

10. Why was the amoeba prison so small?

11. Why couldn't the chicken find her eggs?

12. What does an evil chicken lay?

13. How can you tell a dogwood tree?

14. What did one sheep say to the other sheep?

15. What did the other sheep reply?

16. How many skunks does it take to screw in a light bulb?

17. What is an alligators favorite drink?

18. What would you get if you crossed a trampoline and an iguana?

19. Why did the snake work for the government?

20. Why do birds fly south?

21. How do bloodhounds track down people?

22. Why did the dog have a flat nose?

23. What is another name for a sleeping bull?

24. What is the easiest way to count a heard of cattle?

25. What would you call a cannibal who devoured his mother's sister?

26. What is a hen's favorite book?

27. What do Arabian soldiers use to hide from their enemies?

28. What did they call kittens in the old west?

29. What would you get if you crossed a Chinese cat with an alley cat?

30. What kind of felines like bowling?

31. What would you get if you crossed men's jewelry and a bobcat?

32. What do you get if you crossed a dog and a kangaroo?

33. What would you get if you crossed a stockbroker and an alligator?

34. How did the donkey live?

35. What did prehistoric carpenters use to cut through wood?

36. What is slithery and good at counting?

37. What did the octopus take with him on a camping trip?

38. What is a horse's favorite sport?

39. What's in the middle of a popular horse magazine?

40. What do you call a baby monkey?

41. Where do lambs like to go on vacation?

42. How many insects does it take to make a landlord?

43. Have you heard about the new ant doll?

44. Why did the octopus go to the doctor?

45. What did the baby whale say to its mother?

46. Why did one shrimp crash into another shrimp?

47. Why was a dolphin feeder hired at the zoo?

48. What do whales like to chew?

49. What did the waiter reply when a customer asked for a nice lobster tail?

50. How do fish travel to work?

51. What happened to the woman who had ten children?

52. Where do whales learn how to spell?

53. What did the farmer do when his chickens flew away?

54. What happened to the long-necked bird that was a social outcast?

55. Why doesn't Sweden export cattle?

56. What did the leftover turkey say after it was wrapped up?

57. What do you call a rhino that drinks alcohol?

58. Why did the lamb call the police?

59. What room did the squirrel get at the hotel?

60. Where did the farmer keep his pet seahorse?

61. How do you know that the little snake caught a cold?

62. What did one badger say to the other badger?

63. What is a baby fish's favorite game?

64. What game do young fish like playing?

65. What kind of bats swing upside down?

66. What do you get when you cross a blue jay with a frog

67. Why didn't the church mouse live in the steeple?

68. What would you call a bird that joins the ice capades?

69. Where do woodpeckers conduct their business?

70. How do you make a pig fly?

71. What do kangaroos read?

72. What do you get if you cross and elephant with a model T car?

Silly Questions

1. What do you call a cow that eats your grass?
2. Why is a dog like a telephone?
3. What do you call a dog that likes bubble bath?
4. Why area elephants poor?
5. What is a big as an elephant but weighs nothing?
6. How do you stop an elephant from charging?
7. How do flies travel from place to place?
8. What is the difference in a piano and fish?
9. What did the frog order from the drive-in?
10. What animal never tells the truth?
11. What kind of a key can't open a door?
12. Where did the tiger go when he lost his tail?
13. What do you call a pony with wings?
14. What is the best animal to be on a cold day?
15. What is an owls favorite subject?
16. What is black and white and red all over?
17. How do you keep a skunk from smelling?
18. What is a snake's favorite subject?
19. What is more wonderful than a horse who can count?
20. What is worse than a giraffe with a sore throat?
21. Why are crows the most contented of all birds?
22. Why is a hen immortal?
23. Why do bees hum?
24. Why do white sheep eat more than black sheep?
25. What happens when you illegally park a frog?
26. What do you call a chicken on the go?
27. Why couldn't the animals on Noah's Ark eat apples?
28. What do you call a duck that has lost his job?

Herd About Town

The following game asks you to fill in the blank with the animal whose group is indicated in the accompanying statement or question. Clues are provided throughout the text especially in the group chapter. See how many you can get before you look at the answers.

1. ----- sleep in a water bed.
2. A ----‘- murder is not a crime.
3. ----- make knots without a rope.
4. ------ siege upon each other.
5. An ------‘- spat is not disagreeable.
6. ---- build their colony.
7. ---- use shrewdness in their shrewdness.
8. An ant’s ---- has its own weapons.
9. ------ live in convocation.
10. ------- transact business in a body.
11. ----- attend charm school.
12. You cannot make a sweater from a ----- of geese.
13. ------ enjoy the plague.
14. ------- wish each other happy tidings.
15. ------- richness is togetherness.
16. ------- troop in a troop.
17. A barren of ----- is not barren.
18. -------- in an ostentation are often ostentatious.
19. A bouquet of -------- doesn't qualify as a nose-gay.
20. A ------‘- congregation is not religious.
21. A ------‘- kindle will not start a fire.
22. A --------‘- dray does not have wheels.
23. Turkeys can be in a ------ with their feet on the ground.
24. You can't tie a knot with a ------ of ponies.
25. A rhinoceros ----- is not an accident.
26. A nightingale’s ----- doesn't tick.
27. You can’t ride on a camel’s -----.
28. Ferrets transact -------- in a body.
29. Finches attend ----- school.
30. Locust enjoy the ------.
31. Magpies wish each other happy -------.

32. Martin's -------- doesn't have to do with money.
33. A plover's ------------ is not religious.
34. Sparrows ---- for groups.
35. A giraffe's ----- doesn't transmit
36. You can not rent a room in a beaver's -----.
37. A mussel's ----- is not the same as an Indians.
38. You can't play on a dog's -----.
39. A ------ of deer is not a package.
40. Have you ever seen a deer on a -----?
41. A ------- of ducks doesn't have anything to do with hair.
43. Do fish attend school in -------?
44. A frog can't tie a ---- with a ------ of ponies.
45. A hen's ------- won't start a car (or light a flashlight.)
46. A ---- of leopards is not a jump.
47. An oyster's ---- doesn't handle money.
48. Do swine hear better in a -------?
49. Do turtles ---- hay?
50. A vulture's ---- adds on.

The following statements provide information that may or may not be familiar to you. Fill in the blank with the name of an animal for the correct answer.

Many are in awl of the ---, others don't give a hoot. ----- are said to have tunnel vision and advise it is unwise to badger a ------ or to bully a ---- ---.

The --- --- is a dirty ----.

You can't win the race of life by ------- around. When you ride a ----- do it with care or you could be riding a hearse. Be careful also how you grab a ----, you may get pinched. You will not be able to hold your head high after hearing the protest and dissent should you decide to ----- a -----.

Fighting a ------- can be a thrilla, but you'll go to the ---- if you ------ with him very long. The best formula would be to ---- before he gets a hold of you. Don't volunteer to be a ------ ---on this one. It will cost you more than huffing and ------, one ---- and you could be done for.

Opinions:
-------- are not hampered by their pouch. A ----- will flinch if you pinch its nose. The ---- says you would have to be an --- to look a gift ----- in the mouth unless your a -----.

The --- will pester anyone.

A -------- court decision can do as much harm as a formal sentence.

Many shake when they see a ----- but, need not worry when the -------- is on the loose.

The ------ knows it is necessary to exercise for strength but is not fooled by the morose expression of the -----.

The ----- can not avoid getting caught robbing a worm even after ----ing for excuses. Ask the ------- who knows it doesn't pay to stick your neck out.

Money unlocks the clue for this ------ business and you would pay a lot of ---- for this member of the ------ family with large ears and soft ----. That's something the ---- ----- doesn't have to shed any --------- tears about.

You would need a very large trunk to carry an --------.

The ---- does not peddle its prey, nor does the ---- try to be a hero, both know you can't get ahead by -------. Certainly that wouldn't be -------. ---- and cheating is no laughing matter, as the ----- found out when they got their carcass cleaned on the last killing.

Beware of loan ------, read every word before you ---- the deal. It is better to -------- away enough cash to avoid having any contact with the ------. Most of the time their deal really stinks and these ------- gobble up the best of the bargain.

Epilogue

In summary, animals are more than symbols to man. They have influenced so much that we do.

Consider man's personality traits, especially the desired ones, where animals have led the way. Their courage, commitment and intelligence have motivated man to a higher level of accomplishment. Their companionship has been a comfort in times of loneliness, depression and suffering. Their loyalty devotion, and trust has set the example and their excitement has cheered man to better ways of doing things and to more happiness.

Industriousness is perhaps where animal lessons have had the most impact. Watch a termite build a hill, a beaver construct a dam, a bee labor over a hive, a bird build a nest, or a prairie dog develop a town to appreciate the impact they exerted. Their contribution to our comfort through trailblazing ventilation and air conditioning methods has been an inspiration to builders around the globe. Their dedication and loyalty supporting us when we are feeling poorly is invaluable. Their assistance to our law enforcement agencies and military has been an inspiration to all that serve with them.

Sufficient evidence has been presented to convince even the skeptic that animals have played a significant role in mans development. It is also important to realize many of these instructors have a sense of self and therefore an ego, together with the capacity for superego development within their own breed.

While man's ego may be more developed and complex, many of our animal instructors also possess basic drives and feelings. Animals experience jealousy and guilt, as well as the need to conform, to be accepted, and to seek recognition and status. Their "feelings" have a more consistent tendency as they are not as influenced by changing technology and morals as we humans.

In either case, we should be aware of these traits in animals. It is fitting that we make an effort to nurture their needs not only as a humane thing to do but in recognition of the tremendous contribution animals have made to mankind.

Let us resolve to be more cognizant of their needs.

Glossary

Adapt-to change behavior or adjust needs in order to survive in changing conditions

Aestivation-a sleep similar to hibernation that occurs in hot or dry weather, in ethic animals hide in mud or other places.

Amphibians-animals that are spend most of their tije on land but return to the water to lay eggs I.E. frogs.

Annelid-a type of worm, such as an earthworm, with a soft, rounded body that is made up of segments.

Antenna-a long sensory structure, or feeler, found on the head of an insect, crustaceans, and some other arthropods.

Anthropoid-an animal with jointed limbs and a hard outer-I.E. spider.

Anurans-Amphibians that belong to the order Anurans. Frogs and toads are also members of this group.

Arachnid-an arthropod with four pairs of legs, such as a spider or scorpion.

Arboreal-describes an animal that spends most of its time in trees

Arthropod -an invertebrate, such as an insect, crustacean or arachnid, that has a hard body case and jointed legs.

Bacteria-a group of simple, single-celled organisms, the most abundant on Earth.

Backbone- a series of bones that interconnect to protect the spinal chord that runs down the back connecting the skull.

Binomial name: the two-part Latin name assigned to a species under the system of binomial nomenclature established in the 1700s by Swedish botanist Carl Linnaeus Species. The first name is the name of the genus the species belongs to, the second name is the species name. For example: ***Anolis carolinensis.*** (3)

BioBlitz: an event in which teams of scientists, volunteers, and community members join together to find, identify, and learn about as many local plant and animal species as possible in a set amount of time (often 24 hours). (4)

Biodiversity: the variety of all living things (species), including plants, animals, microorganisms; their interrelationships; the genes they contain; and, the ecosystems they form.

Bivalve-a shell divided into two, bivalve mollusks include mussels and clams.

Browser-an animal that feeds on the leaves of trees and bushes.

Calcium carbonate-a white, solid mineral salt that forms or reinforces the shells of mollusks and the cuticle of crustaceans.

Carcass-the body of a dead animal.

Carnassials-a type of tooth, found in flesh-eating animals, that is designed to cut-up meat in guillotine fashion.

Carapace-the hard shield that covers and protects the head and thorax if crustaceans such as lobsters and crabs.

Carnivores-meat eating animals.

Carrion-the bodies of animals that have died naturally or been killed by other animals.

Cephalopod-a type of mollusk, such as an octopus, that has a distinct head with large eyes and testacies with suckers.

Cephalpod-a marine mollusk characterized by well-developed head and eyes and sucker-bearing tentacles-relating to Cephalopoda

Cephalothorax-the anterior of any one of the Arachnida and higher Crustacea, consisting of the united head and thorax.

Cervids-a group of ungulates which includes deer and antelopes

Chordate-a member of a group of animals that includes vertebrates, such as fish and reptiles.

Classification: Taxonomic classification refers to the organization of organisms by traits, such as size, color, or form, or by their degree of genetic relatedness. Most scientists have agreed on a scheme that classifies all life on Earth into three Domains; each Domain is further divided into Kingdoms, Phyla, Classes, Orders, Families, Genera, and Species.

Cocoon-a community where all members live and work together.

Coral-small animals that live in large groups, or colonies in the sea. A coral reef is made up of the hard skeletons of coral animals.

Counter shading-coloring in which the underside, normally in shadow, is paler than the side that is exposed to the light.

Crepuscular-referring to an animal that is active between the hours of twilight and dawn.

Crustaceans- animals with a hard, jointed outer shell that lives mostly in water. Lobsters, crabs, and shrimp are examples.

Cryptic camouflage-camouflage that disguises the shape of the animal

Diurnal-animals that sleep at night and are active during the day.

Domain: A taxonomic classification category above Kingdom. The three domains are Archaea, Bacteria and Eukaryota. (See Classification).

Echinoderm-a marine invertebrat, such as a starfish or sea urchin, with an internal skeleton and a body divided into five equal parts.

Ecology-the study of the interrelationships among plants, animals and other organisms and their interaction with all aspects of their natural environment.

Ecosystem-a community of plants, animals and microorganisms that are linked by energy and nutrient flows and that interact with each other and with the physical environment. Rainforests, deserts, coral reefs, grasslands and rotting saguaro cactus are all examples of ecosystems.

Echolocation-used by bats and whales to help them find prey. The animal makes a high-pitched sound and then uses the echoes that bounce off any object in its path to work out where and how big that object is.

Exothermic -an animal whose body temperature depends on the temperature of the environment around it.

Endangered-species that are those whose numbers are declining because of over-hunting, loss of habitat etc,

Endemic-referring to an animal that is typical and exclusive to a given place. Lemurs, for example, are endemic to Madagascar.

Endothermic-describes an anima, such as a frog or snake, whose internal temperature varies with that of the external temperature.

Environment-the surroundings in which plants and animals live.

Enzyme-a substance that speeds up chemical reactions-including the break down of food molecules during digestion-inside animals and other organisms.

Evolution-a process in which the animals that survive to reproduce are the ones that are the fittest and the strongest.

Excrete- to get rid of waste fro an animal's body.

Extinct- describes a species of animal that is no longer inexistence

Fauna- The animals found in a given area.

Flora- The plants found in a given area.

Folivore-an animal that feeds on fruit.

Fossils-the remains of plants or animals from an earlier time period that are found in rock or it Earth's crust.

Fungus- (pl fungi)-a primitive plant that cannot make its own food ad must live on food made by other organs, living or dead.

Gene-a section of a chromosome containing enough DNA to control the formation of one protein; a gene controls the transmission of a hereditary character.

Gene pool-the total number of genes (or alleles) in a population of organisms.

Gill-a structure found in fish and other aquatic animals, used for taking in oxygen and releasing carbon dioxide under water.

Gonad-an organ, such as the testis or ovary, that produces sex cells used in reproduction.

Grazer-an animal that feeds on grasses.

Habitat: The place or environment where a plant or animal naturally lives and grows; a group of particular environmental conditions.

Herbivores-plant eaters.

Hibernation-a state of rest or inactivity in which most bodily functions such as hear beat and breathing, slow down.

Indicator species-a species whose presence or absence is known to be indicative of a particular habitat or environmental condition. (1)

Indigenous species-a species that occurs naturally in an area or habitat. A species that originated in, and grows or lives naturally in a particular region or environment.

Insects-invertebrates with a three segmented body (head, thorax abdomen), a hard outer shell and 6-legs" I.E. grasshopper, butterflies, dragon flies.

Instinct-a behavior pattern that is inborn, not learned.

Introduced species-a species that has been transported by humans across a geographic barrier to a location where it previously did not exist. Introduced species can compete with and cause problems for native species, i.e. become invasive exotic species.

Invasive species-an aggressive alien species that displaces native species; most commonly in disturbed habitats, although the most destructive invasive species also displace natives in intact communities.

Invertebrates-animals that do not have a back bone.

Keystone species-a species that exerts a major influence on the composition and dynamics of the community in which it lives; species which influence many other by their presence.

Krill-a shrimp-like crustacean that forms the main food source of baleen whales.

Larva (pl larvae)-the wingless, wormlike form of a newly hatched insect; the stage after the egg but before full development.

Life cycle-the span of the life of an organism, from the moment of fertilization (or asexual generation) to the time it reproduces.

Mammals-ani8mals that are fur bearing or have hair, and feed their young milk I.E. humans, bear.

Marsupial-a kind of mammal that gives birth to very small, immature young which are then carried in a pouch on the female's body while they grow.

Metamorphosis-a complete change in form or appearance; in most insects, this change occurs in stages: egg, larva, pupa, and adult.

Micro-organisms: Any organism that can be seen only with the aid of a microscope.

Migrate-to move from one place or climate to another, usually on a seasonal basis.

Mimicry-when harmless animals use superficial means to secure their protection-they employ color, sound, imitation, camouflage, and other means in their deception.

Model organism-a model organism is a non-human species that is widely studied and used to understand particular biological functions or systems

Mollusks--animals with a hard, outer shell, usually living in water such as clams and snails.

Musekids-musk bearing animals.

Mustelids include such animals as weasels, skunks, badgers, ferrets, and others.

Natural selection-the natural process by which biological traits that affect survival and/or reproduction become more or less common in a population. Population-any group of conspecific organisms coexisting at the same time and in the same place and capable of interbreeding with one another.

Nectar-a sweet liquid found in many flowers, often used as a food source by insects.

Nocturnal-animals that sleep during the day and are active at night- I. E. rabbits, owls.

Nourishment-any substance that helps an animal grow, develop, and survive: food.

Nurse-to drink milk from the mother's body.

Nymph-a stage in the life cycle of certain insects. Nymphs look like smaller wingless versions of adults insect.

Omnivore-an animal that mainly eats all kinds of things, including plants and animals.

Organism-a living thing (plant, animal, or microbe).

Parasite-an animal that lives on or inside the body of another animal and depends on it for food.

Pheromone-a chemical message released by an animal that has an effect on other members of its species.

Plantigrade- a term that refers to an animal that walks with the entire soles of its feet on the ground. Human beings and bears are plantigrade animals.

Plankton-tiny plants and animals that live in water. Most can only be seen through a microscope.

Plants: A member of the kingdom Plantae. Characterized by being multicellular, having cells specialized as distinct tissues, and gaining its nutrition by photosynthesis. (1)

Pollution-poisoning the air and water with smoke, oil, harmful chemicals, and other industrial waste.

Polyp-a small barrel-shaped animal, such as a sea anemone or coral, with a mouth surrounded by testacies at the top end.

Predators-animals that hunt and eat other animals.

Prehensile-a part of an animal's body, such as a tail, that can grasp things. Some snakes have a prehensile tail, which they use like an extra limb to hold on to branches.

Prey-animals hunted and eaten by other animals.

Primates-a group of highly advanced mammals; of which man is a member.

Protective coloring-coloring that helps an animal blend into its surroundings so that it escapes the notice of predators or prey.

Pupa-the third stage in the life-cycle of most insects, between larva and adult

Refuse-the place of safety.

Reptiles-animals covered with a protective covering of scales or plates; I.E. crocodiles, alligators, lizards and snakes.

Reproduction-the stages of a life cycle; the way that animals have babies

Savanna-a flat landscape, usually covered with coarse grasses and scattered trees.

Scavenger-an animal that feeds on the remains of creatures that have died naturally or been killed by other eaters.

Rodent-a member of the mammal group Rodentia, which includes rate, mice, and squirrels.

Savannah-a grassland habitat with widely spaced trees found in hotter regions of the world, notably in parts of Africa.

Secrete-to give off substance, usually liquid.

Sericulture-the cultivation of silk, a fiber made from the cocoons of the moth.

Species-animals or plants that are closely related and often similar in behavior and appearance. Members of the same species are capable of breeding together.

Symbiosis-a close relationship between members of two different species that may be mutually beneficial or one-sided.

Talon-the sharp claw of an animal, such as an eagle.

Taxon-plural: taxa-any group or rank in a biological classification into which related organisms are classified.; or (2) A taxonomic unit in the biological system of classification of organisms, for example: a phylum, order, family, genus, or species.

Taxonomy-the science of naming and classifying organisms.

Temperate climate-the climate zones lying between the tropics and the polar regions, with warm summers and cold winters.

Tentacle-the long body parts of an animal; such as a squid.

Tuber-a swelling in the root system of some plants, where food is stored.

Ungulates-animals with hooves, they can be divided into two orders, the Artiodactyls, or even toed ungulates, which includes goats, cows, deer, hippos, and pigs; and Perissodactyls or odd-toed ungulates, which includes horses, tapirs, and rhinoceros

Venom-the poisonous fluid injected by some snakes and scorpions when they bite or sting.

Vertebrates-animals with backbones

Wattle-the fleshy flap on the head or neck of some birds.

Appendix

Holidays

Perhaps attesting to the many contributions of animals to mankind, holidays are named in their honor. The number of the days they can claim as their own is a credit to the contributions they have made and continues to grow. The list below attests to the popularity of this way of recognizing the importance of the kingdom's leadership toward making life easier for all of us.

January
Bald Eagle Appreciation Days
Penguin Awareness Day
Rattlesnake Round Up
Squirrel Appreciation Day

February
National Justice for Animals Week
Homes for Birds Week
Great Backyard Bird Count
Champion Crab Races Day
Cow Milked While Flying in an Airplane Day
Groundhog Day
National Hippo
Serpent Day
National Polar Bear Day
World Whale Day
Cordova Ice Worm Day

March
Prevention of cruelty of animal's month

Aardvark, National Aardvark Week
Learn About Butterflies Day
Buzzard Day
Dolphin Awareness Month
World Frog Day
Adopt a Rescued Guinea Pig Month
National Horse Protection Day \
Manatee Appreciation Day April
International Festival of Owls
National Pig Day
International Day of the Seal
Save a Spider Day
Termite awareness week
Turkey Vultures Return to the Living Sign
National Wildlife Week

April
Bat Appreciation Week-
National Animal Advocacy Day -
World Laboratory Animal Liberation Week
World Week for Animals in Laboratories
International Beaver Day
National Birding Day
National Dolphin Day
Save the Elephant Day
National Ferret Day
Save the Frogs Day)
National Help a Horse Day
World Penguin Day
World Rat Day
Zoo Lovers Day -

May
Be Kind to Animals Week
World Migratory Bird Day
International Respect for Chickens Day
Dinosaur Day

Endangered Species Day
Pink Flamingo Day
International Hug Your Ca
Frog Jumping Jubilee Day
National Pet Week
Save the Rhino Day International Turtle Day
Slugs Return to Capistrano Day
Whooping Crane Day

June
Animal Rights Awareness Week
National Black Cow Day
National Dairy month
International Day of Action for Elephants in Zoos
Pet Appreciation Week World Sea Turtle Day
World Sea Turtle Day
Zoo and Aquarium Month

July
Don't Step on a Bee Day
National Bison Month
Coral Reef Awareness Week
Cow Appreciation Day
I Love Horses Day
Monkey Day
Mosquito Day
Adopt a Rescued Rabbit Month
Rat Catcher's Day
Shark Awareness Day
World Snake Day
Wild About Wildlife Month
American Zoo Day

August
International Assistance Dog Week
International Homeless Animals Day
World Elephant Day

World Lizard Day
World Mosquito Day
World Orangutan Day
Shark Week
International Whale Shark Day

September
World Animal Remembrance Month
Elephant Appreciation Day
National Farm Animals Awareness Week
Fish Amnesty Day
Happy Goose Day
National Hummingbird Day
National Iguana Awareness Day
Save the Koala Month
World Rhino Day
Sea Otter Awareness Week
International Rabbit Day
Shamu the Whale Day
National Wildlife Day

October
National Animal Safety and Protection Month
Animal Welfare Week
World Animal Month
Bat Appreciation Month
Butterfly and Hummingbird Day
World Farm Animals Day
Feral Hog Month, or Hog Out
National Mule Day
International Raccoon
Reptile Awareness Day
Squirrel Awareness Month
National Wolf Awareness Week

November
National Animal Shelter and Rescue Appreciation

National Hug a Bear Day
Jellyfish Day
Manatee Awareness Month

December
National Day of Animal Rights
Christmas Bird Count
National Day of the Horse
Monkey Day
World Wildlife Conservation Day
Visit the Zoo Day

Animals that have a holiday named in their honor.

Aardvark
Ant
Bat
Bear
Beaver
Bee
Birds
Buffalo
Buzzard
Cow
Crab
Dolphin
Eagle
Elephant
Feral hog
Ferret
Frog
Ground Hog
Guinea Pig
Hippopotamus
Horse
Ice Worm
Iguana

Jellyfish
Koala Bear
Lizard
Manatee
Monkey
Mosquito
Mule
Orangutan
Owl
Pig
Polar Bear
Rat
Rattle Snake
Sea Otter
Seal
Shark
Slug
Squirrel
Spider
Termite
Turkey
Whale
Whopping Crane

Answers

Homonym answers-see quiz @Language

1. does doze
2. hoarse horse
3. ant aunt
4. boar bore
5. whale wail
6. hare hair
7. foul fowl
8. gorilla guerrilla
9. dear deer
10. mouse mousse
11. towed toad
12. cheap cheep
13. lynx links
14. lox locks
15. mussel
16. grisly grizzly
17. flees fleas
18. mule mewl
19. new gnu
20. ewes use
21. paws pause
22. roe row
23. herd heard
24. tail tale
25. mite might
26. dual duel

27. meet meat

Group Matching answers-see quiz (@Group

1. Beaver	m. society
2. Bees	h. fry
3. Camels	b. caravan
4. Crocodiles	a. bask
5. Donkeys	l. race
6. Ducks	k. paddling
7. Elk	i. gang
8. Giraffe	p. tower
9. Grasshoppers	c. cloud
10. Guinea fowl	d. confusion
11. Hares	e. down
12. Horses	n. stable
13. Larks	f. exaltation
14. Moles	j. labor
15 Ponies	o. string
16. Termites	q. wood
17. Woodcocks	g. fall

Fowl Play – for answers see story in Group

1. buzzards	1&2 flight
2. vultures	
3. crows	3. murder
4. crocodile	4&5 bask
5. gator	
6. caterpillars	6. army
7. sparrows	7. host
8. jays	8. band
9. swans	9. wedge
10. starlings	10 chattering
11. giraffes	11. tower

12. pigeons
13. turkeys
14. mice
15. geese
16. oyster
17. elk
18. hares
19. rhinoceros
20. cats
21. dogs
22. sardines
23. guinea fowl
24. hound
25. elephant
26. bees
27. sheep
28. ewe
29. locust
30. red deer
31. ponies
32. fox
33. goats
34. mules
35. nightingales
36. jelly fish
37. woodpeckers
38. wolves
39. swallows
40. leopards
41. magpie
42. seal
43. lapwings
44. frogs
45. hens
46. lions
47. toad
48. ants

12. loft
13. rafter
14. nests
15. gaggle
16. spat
17. gang
18. down
19. crash
20. litter
21. pack
22. family
23. confusion
24. cry
25. herd
26. swarm
27. & 28. Flock

29. plague
30. game
31. string
32. skulk
33. trip
34. barren
35. watch
36. smack
37. decent
38. route
39. flight
40. leap
41. tidings
42. & 43. harem, pod

44. deceit
45. brood
46. pride
47. knob
48. colony

49. termites
50. trout
51. ducks
52. mallards
53. whales
54. dolphins
55. mackerel
56. otter
57. auk
58. walrus
59. swans
60. goldfish
61. snakes
62. raven
63. finches
64. fish
65. plovers
66. rook
67. eagles
68. porcupine
69. owls
70. hawks
71. perch
72. monkey
73. peacock
74. swine
75. boars
76. apes
77. robin
78. swift
79. squirrels
80. oxen
81. heron
82. lions
83. turtles
84. ferrets
85. horse

49. wood
50. hover
51. paddling
52. sord
53. mob
54. team
55. shoal
56. raft
57. huddle
58. drift
59. drift
60. troubling
61. bed
62. kindness
63. charm
64. school
65. congregation
66. building
67. convocation
68. parliament
69. cast
70. park
71. tribe
72. muster
73. sounder
74. singular
75. shrewdness
76. dray
77. drove
78. siege
79. troop
80. dole
81. business
82. stable
83. caravan
84. race
85. walk

86. camels
87. donkeys
88. snails
89. skunks
90. tigers
91. flamingos
92. hares
93. prairie dogs
94. bull
95. moles
96. kangaroo
97. tortoise
98. hare
99. rabbit
100. turtle
101. wolves
102. albatross
103. crow

86. chine
87. ambush
88. & 89. trace/down
90. town
91. & 92. labor/movement
93. troop
94. bale
95. warren
96. warren
97. bale
98. rook
99.
100.
101.
102.
103. murder

Animal Crackers answers-see quiz @Games

1. Horse
2. Doe and Bucks
3. A Seal
4. A Bat (yes a bat is an animal)
5. Bear (bear)
6. Cheetah (cheater)
7. Hare (hair)
8. A good steer
9. Deer
10. Boar
11. A hog, because he has a hogshead full of them.
12. Because he always has his back up.
13. When it's U, dear
14. Your Calves

15. Reindeer (rain dear)
16. A little Otter (hotter)
17. A Cow because it always wants to eat its fodder (father)
18. A led (lead) horse
19. A road Hog

Bird Bafflers answers-see quiz (@Games

1. Jay
2. Swallow
3. Cardinal
4. Rook
5. Tern (turn)
6. Loons and cuckoos
7. Robin
8. Rail
9. Crane
10. Mockingbird
11. Because the have a high time after dark.
12. By giving their notes.
13. When it's a tumbler.
14. Bluebird

Common terms answers-see question (@Games

ALL ARE HORSE-DRAWN VEHICLES

Cows and Gators answers-see quiz (@Games

1. milk shakes
2. condensed milk
3. milk of amnesia
4. evaporated milk
5. vanishing cream
6. cold cream

7. cream of wit
8. because they are often in a bad moo-ed
9. herdly ever
10. del-egators (deli-gators)
11. congre-gators
12. navigators
13. investigators
14. croco-dials

Catching fish answers-see quiz (@Games

1. Flounder
2. Shark
3. Goldfish
4. Dogfish
5. Kingfish
6. Angelfish
7. Drumfish
8. Buffalo fish
9. Hagfish
10. Catfish
11. Perch
12. Butterfish
13. Pike
14. Bass
15. Grunt
16. Sailfish
17. Fantail
18. Swordfish
19. Starfish
20. Weakfish
21. Jellyfish
22. Devilfish
23. Backfish
24. Balloon fish
25. Cow fish
26. Red snapper

27. Cod (c.o.d.)
28. Smelt
29. Blue fish
30. Sunfish

Hink-Pink answers

1. Owl towel
2. Thrush brush
3. Hawk talk
4. Swallow swallow
5. Dipper dipper
6. Pigeon pidgin
7. Wren yen
8. Tern turn
9. Grouse spouse
10. Trumpeter trumpeter
11. Rail jail
12. Hawk squawk
13. Thrush brush
14. Robin bobbin
15. Crane cane
16. Finch stinch
17. Stork fork
18. Wren glen
19. Finch flinch
20. Crow show
21. Crow glow
22. Raven haven
23. Fowl owl
24. Swift swift
25. Turtle hurdle
26. Turkey jerky
27. Wet pet
28. Gater freighter
29. Impala impala
30. Gnu zoo

31. Bongo bongo
32. Gnu zoo
33. Gnu ewe
34. Rare bear
35. Beaver cleaver
36. Lone drone
37. Wee bee
38. Dull gull
39. Vulture culture
40. Quail sale
41 Kite bite
42. Egret regret
43. Vain crane
44. Crow glow
45. Gull skull
46. Tit fit
47. Puffin muffin
48. Loon tune
49. Flicker snicker
50. Croaker poker
51. Gar jar
52. Loach poach
53. Carp tarp
54. Sturgeon surgeon
55. Pike hike
56. Weever weaver
57. Perch church
58. Mullet gullet
59. Mod cod
60. Runt grunt
61. Biting whiting
62. Serene sardine
63. Odd cod
64. Sole sole
65. Bad shad
66. Kipper zipper
67. Selfish shellfish

68. Fish dish
69. Frog log
70. Road toad
71. Nanny nanny
72. Gander gander
73. Gaggle waggle
74. Loose goose
75. Quail sale
76. Partridge cartridge
77. Gibbon ribbon
78. Chimp blimp
79. Gorilla guerilla
80. Ape cape
81. Kite fight
82. Pig wig
83. Hack hack
84. Seed feed
85. Hag gag
86. Nag flag
87. Colt molt
88. Phony pony
89. Gay bay
90. Cavalier cavalier
91. Silly filly
92. Gay neigh
93. Sable stable
94. Horse
95. Ant grant
96. Bug rug
97. Bug hug
98. Bee knee
99. Flea glee
100. Bug drug
101. Fat gnat
102. Llama drama
103. Lemur femur
104. Skink stink

105. Mink sink
106. Mole mole
107. Mole hole
108. Mink shrink
109. Chimp blimp
110. Moose mousse
111. Miller killer
112. Vole role
113. House mouse
114. Nice mice
115. Verbal gerbil
116. Gopher loafer
117. Otter spotter
118. Sow row
119. Tapir paper
120. Boar sore
121. Big pig
122. Fine swine
123. Noon coon
124. Bunny money
125. Hare liar
126. Bunny gunny
127. Hare snare
128. Funny bunny
129. Bare hare
130. Square hare
131. Rabbit habit
132. Lamb tram
133. Sheep weep
134. Cheap sheep
135. Krill grille
136 Drunk skunk
137. Snail veil
138. Snail trail
139. Snake ache
140. Mamba samba
141. Asp gasp

142. Viper snipe
143. Snake ache
144. Rattler battler
145. Snake shake
146. Snake stake
147. Spider cider
148. Turkey jerky
149. Turtle hurtle
150. Hornet cornet
151. Ermine vermin
152. Mod pod
153. Whale jail

Riddle answers-see questions (@Games

1. The aardvarks and the aaren'tvarks.
2. Ant-chovies.
3. Peanut butter-flies.
4. A small bee in a big hive.
5. A fumble bee.
6. In the ark-hives.
7. Corn on the cob.
8. With bull point pens.
9. Tweetment.
10. Because it had only one cell.
11. Because she mislaid them.
12. Deviled eggs.
13. By its bark.
14. "After ewe."
15. "Thank ewe."
16. Quite a phew!
17. Gator-ade.
18. Leaping lizards.
19. He wanted to be in a civil serpent.
20. A bear mid-drift.
21. Because it's too far to walk
22. He liked chasing parked cars.

23. A bulldozer
24. Use a cowculator
25. An aunt-eater.
26. "Great Eggspectations" by Charles Chickens.
27. Camelflage.
28. Posse cats.
29. A Peking Tom.
30. Alley cats.
31. Cuff lynx
32. A pooch with a pouch.
33. An investigator.
34. On burro'd time.
35. Dinosaws.
36. An adder.
37. Tent-acles.
38. Stable tennis.
39. A monthly center foal.
40. A chip off the old block.
41. To the Baaahamas.
42. Ten-ants
43. You wind it up and it goes on a picnic.
44. Because he was a crazy mixed-up squid.
45. "I don't feel whale."
46. It was accident prawn.
47. To serve a porpoise.
48. Blubber gum.
49. "Once upon a time there was a nice lobster"
50. In carp pools.
51. She went stork raving mad.
52. In the Moby Dicktionary.
53. He tried to recoop (recoup) his losses.
54. It was ostrichized.
55. Because it wants to keep its Stockholm.
56. "Foiled again."
57. A win-oceros.
58. He had been fleeced.
59. The nutcracker suite.

60. In the barn-acle.
61. Because she adder viper nose.
62. "Too badger sick."
63. Salmon says.
64. Carps and robbers.
65. Acro-bats
66. The bluebird of hoppiness.
67. She didn't a-spire that high.
68. A cheep skate.
69. In branch offices.
70. Add e-o-n to its name and it turns into a pigeon.
71. Pocketbooks.
72. Either a cranky elephant or a car with a very large trunk.

Silly Questions answers

1. A lawn mooer
2. It has collar I.D
3. A sham-poodle
4. Because the work for peanuts
5. His shadow
6. Take away its credit card
7. They itch-hike
8. You can tuna fish
9. Flies and a croak
10. lion
11. A monkey
12. Retailer
13. A horse fly
14. A little otter
15. Owlgebra
16. An embarrassed penguin
17. Plug up his nose
18. History
19. A Spelling bee
20. A centipede with flat feet.
21. Because they never complain without caws.

22. Because her son never sets.
23. Because they don't know the words.
24. There are so many more white sheep.
25. It gets toad away.
26. Poultry in motion.
27. Only pears where let on board
28. A fired cracker.

Group fill in the blank answers -see fill-in-blanks (@Games

1. Clams
2. Crows
3. Frogs
4. Heron's
5. Oyster
6. Ants
7. Ape's
8. Army
9. Eagle's
10. Ferret
11. Finch
12. Skein
13. Locust
14 Magpies
15 Martin's
16. Monkey's
17. Mules
18. Peacocks
19. Pheasant
20. Plovers
21. Kitten
22. Squirrel
23. Rafter
24. String
25. Crash
26. Watch
27. Train

28. Business
29. Charm
30. Plague
31. Tidings
32. Richness
33. Congregation
34. Host
35. Tower
36. Lodge
37. Scalp
38. Bench
39. Parcel
40. Leash
41. Balding
42. Schools
43. Knot/string
44. Battery
45. Leap
46. Bank
47. Sounder
48. Bank
49. Bale
50. Peal

Animal Activity answers-see quiz (@Games

Many are in awl of the OWL, others don't give a hoot. MOLES are said to have tunnel vision and advise it is unwise to badger a BADGER or to bully a BULL DOG.

The MUD HEN is a dirty BIRD.

You can't win the race of life by HORSING around. When you ride a HORSE do it with care or you could be riding a hearse. Be careful also how you grab a CRAB, you may get pinched.

Fighting a GORILLA can be a thrilla, but you'll go to the DOGS if you MONKEY with him very long. The best formula would be to FLEA before he gets a hold of you. Don't volunteer to be a GUINEA PIG on this one. It will cost you more than huffing and PUFFIN; one SLUG and you could be done for.

Opinions:

HAMSTERS are not hampered by their pouch.

A FINCH will flinch if you pinch its nose.

The MULE says you would have to be an ASS to look a gift HORSE in the mouth unless you're a HORSE.

The BUG will pester anyone.

A KANGAROO court decision can do as much harm as a formal sentence.

Many shake when they see a SNAKE, but need not worry when the MONGOOSE is on the loose.

The MUSSEL knows it is necessary to exercise for strength but is not fooled by the morose expression of the MOOSE.

The ROBIN can not avoid getting caught robbing a worm even after FISHing for excuses. Ask the GIRAFFE who knows, it doesn't pay to stick your neck out.

Money unlocks the clue for this MONKEY business and you would pay a lot of JACK for this member of the RABBIT family with large ears and soft HARE. That's something the BALD EAGLE doesn't have to shed any CROCODILE tears about.

You would need a very large trunk to carry an ELEPHANT.

Herd About Town

The HAWK does not peddle its prey, nor does the HERON try to be a hero, both know you can't get ahead by CHEETAH. Certainly that wouldn't be CRICKET. LION and cheating is no laughing matter, as the HYENA found out when they got their carcass cleaned on the last killing.

Beware of loan SHARKS, read every word before you SEAL the deal. It is better to SQUIRREL away enough cash to avoid having any contact with the SKUNKS. Most of the time their deal really stinks and these TURKEYS gobble up the best of the bargain.

Bibliography

Ammer, Christine. *Cool Cats, Top Dogs and Other Beastly Expressions* Hougton Mifflin Company. Boston, Massachusetts 1999

Anselm, Virgilius Ture. *Lightening Never Strikes Twice* Gramacy Publishing Co. 225 Park Ave South, NY 1987

Barkin, Carol and Elizabeth James. The Holiday Handbook Clarion Books 1994

Barre,' Michael. *How Animals Protect Themselves* Gareth Stevens Publishing Milwaukee, Wisconsin 1998

Bartlett, John & Justin Kaplan, *Bartlett's Familiar Quotations*, Little Brown and Company Boston, Toronto, London 1992

Boysen, Dr. Sally. *The Smartest Animals on the Planet* Firefly Books Buffalo, New York and Richmond Hill Onterio, Canada 2009

Brandreth, Giles. *The Joy of Lex,* Gary and Morris William Morrow & Company London 1983

Browne, Philippa-Alys. *A Gaggle of Geese: the collective names of the animal kingdom*

Carl, Jean. *Atheneum Books for Young Readers* Simon Schuster New York 1961

Cole, William. An *Arkful of Animals* Houghton Miffin New York 1978

Collins, Rex. *A Crash of Rhinoceros* Moyer Bell Wakefiels, Rhode Island & London 1993

Breland, Osmond. *Animal Friends and Foes* P. Harper New York & London 1957

Coston, Bruce R. *Ask the Animals* Martins Press New York 2009

Dembeck, Herman. *Animals and Men* Natural History Press Garden City, NY 1965

Espy Willard R. A Children's Almanac of Words at Play. Clarkson Porter Publishing Clarkson, GA 1988

Feldman, David. *Who Put the Butter in Butterfly* Harper and Row New

York1990
Feldman, David. New York *When do Fish Sleep* Harpers and Roe Publishers New York 1989
Fox, Michael W.D., Sc., PH.D., B. Med., M.R.C.V.S.*Between Animal and Man* Coward, McCann & Geoghegan, Inc. New York 1976
Funk, Charles Earle. A Hog on Ice and Other Curious Expressions 2002
Gorge, Jean Craighead. *The First Thanksgiving* Philomel Books New York 1971
Grant, James R. & Carol. *Animal Architects* Gould Basic Books New York, New York 2007
Hatch, Jane M. American Book of Days Hw Wilson Company New York 1978
Heller, Ruth. *A Cache of Jewels and Other Collective Nouns*,; Scholastic Press New York 1989
Hendrickson, Robert. *Animal Crackers* Viking Press New York 1983
Herrod, James. All Things great and Small St. Martins Press New York 1972
Hornblow, Leonora & Arthur. Animals Do the Strangest Things Random House New York 1965
Lamb ,G. F. *Animal Quotations*. Longman Dictionaries Europe 1985
Lederer, Richard, A Man of My Words St. Martin Press New York 2003
Lederer, Richard. *The Play of Words*, Pocket Books London, Toronto, New York, Syndey,
Lederer, Richard. *Get Thee to a Punnery* Wyrick & Company Charleston, SC 1988
Lipton, James. *An Exaltation of Larks* Grossman Publishers New York 1977
Lyman, Darryl. *Dictionary of Word and Phrase Origins*, Jonathan David Publisher Mc Kinnon, Elizabeth. ASDC *Special Day Celebrations* Warren Publishing House, Inc Everett, Washington 1989
Mac Carthy, Patricia. *Herds of Words* Dial Books for Young Readers; New York 1991
Masson, Jeffrey Moussaieff. Beast Bloomsbury New York, London, New Delhi, Sydney 2014
Morris, Desmond. *Animal Watching* Random House 1New York 1994
Morris, Rick. *Mysteries & Marvels of Nature* Usborne Publishing Ltd. Europe 1989
Newkirk, Ingrid. *Save the Animals* Warner Books Hatchette Book Group1990
Perry, Kate. *Animal Camouflage & Defense* Chelsea House Publishing London, England 2005
Peters, John O., *Hollywood Cemetery*, Richmond History Center 2010

Pim, Paul. Telling Tommy about Days We Celebrate Cupples and Leon New York 1941

Potter, Carole. *Knock on Wood & other Superstitions* Sammis Publishing Corporation.-Bonanza Books NY 1984

Racinelli, Maria, *Animal Mimicry* Power Kids Press New York 2010

Racinelli, Maria. *Animals with Armor Power Kids Press New York 2010*

Sarnoff, Jane and Reynold Ruffins. *If You were Really Superstitious* -1980 Charles Scribner's Sons NY

Sarnoff, Jane and Reynold Ruffins. *Take Warning A Book of Superstitions* Charles Scribner's Sons NY 1980

Saxon, Gladys R. *Origin of Animal Names*: Secrets of Animals Names -. -Prentice Hall New York 1964

Seabury, Edna Bartth. *Reindeer and Colored Lig*hts Press 1971

Sparks, John. *Discovery of Animal Behavior* Arrow Books Ltd. 1991

Stewart, Ian. *The Mathematics of Life* Basic Books NY 2011

Turlin, Melissa S. *Aardvarks to Zebras* Citadel Press New York 1995

Uhlenbroek, Charlotte. *Animal Life Darling* Kindersley Limited-London, New York, Melbourne. Munich and Delhi 2008

Walker, Richard. *Animal Life* Darling Kindersley Limited-London, New York, Melbourne, Munich and Delhi 2009

Walters, Martin. *Book of Animals* Farrar Straus Giroux of McMillan New 2001

About the Author

Bob Layton, a resident of Glen Allen, Virginia, retired from a successful insurance sales career in 1993. During his tenure, he served as president of the both the Richmond and Virginia Life Underwriters Associations and served on several national committees. He was also the lobbying arm of the state association for a number of years and a life member of the Million Dollar Roundtable.

In retirement, Bob has found a variety of life's fun things to do. His interests range from volunteering, traveling, writing and reading to an occasional political dabble. Bob has written more than 150 articles on a variety of subjects with thirty-five different publications. His play George Washington Wept Here has not met expectations but was a rewarding activity.

Robert C. Layton

The research for putting pen to paper has provided the material for his more than two hundred lectures on travel, history, monuments and animals. He has appeared before a variety of audiences giving programs in national parks, retirement facilities, libraries and historical societies, as well as for Elderhostel and at the University of Richmond. He numbers teaching sixth grade in Beijing, China, as one of the most rewarding retirement experiences.

Bob has traveled to all fifty states and visited more than seventy-five countries. Walking across the Grand Canyon, climbing the Great Wall of China and weekly tennis has contributed to an exciting withdrawal from the workplace.

About the Cover Designer

Whether it's design, illustration or photography, Aaron is passionate about visual communication and expression. After earning a BFA in Graphic Design from James Madison University, Aaron started his career at one of the top design firms in Richmond, VA, where he worked with a diverse group of local and national clients. Along the way, he learned a great deal about print production, time management and how to work well with clients, vendors and other designers.

Since founding 903 Creative with his wife in 2008, Aaron has had the opportunity to design for start-ups, non-profits, Fortune 500s, and world-touring musicians.

He has experience with a wide range of projects from identity design and brand development to print and web design. His work has been recognized by AIGA (the professional association for design) and included in several leading international design publications.

When not designing, Aaron enjoys finding new ways to grow creatively, traveling the world with this wife & children and strolling their historic neighborhood streets with the family beagle, Daisy.